SOFT HOUSE

SOFT HOUSE

by Steve Futterman

illustrated by Margot Apple

& edited by Nina Miller

Harper & Row, Publishers

New York, Hagerstown, San Francisco, London

FIRST EDITION

Library of Congress Catalog Card Number: 75—23881

ISBN: 0—06—011386—3

Designed by Janice Willcocks Stern

76 77 78 79 80 10 9 8 7 6 5 4 3 2 1

dedicated to the preservation of nomads & wild places

CONTENTS

INTRODUCTION

Soft houses have been around for thousands of years, and with the climbing cost of hard-house construction, I'm not surprised at their rapid comeback.

When I started camping, there was no large-scale hiking and camping industry. The equipment consisted of what was at hand. By trial and error, I found out what worked and what didn't.

At present there are about five million active campers in the United States, and nearly twenty million more thinking about it. There is a dazzling amount of gear available to them from hundreds of sources. However, the majority of potential campers don't know enough about these products to choose the right ones.

In my travels, I have heard many of the same questions asked over and over again. This book of personal experiences is an answer to some of them.

see you in the woods,
Steve & Winnie

✩

A sampling of soft houses that
were in use yesterday, today, and
hopefully tomorrow. The last
four designs are mine and are
not available commercially. However,
you can execute any design your
mind can envision with needle,
thread, and sensitivity.

MOUNTAIN TENT

2-person high-altitude expedition type

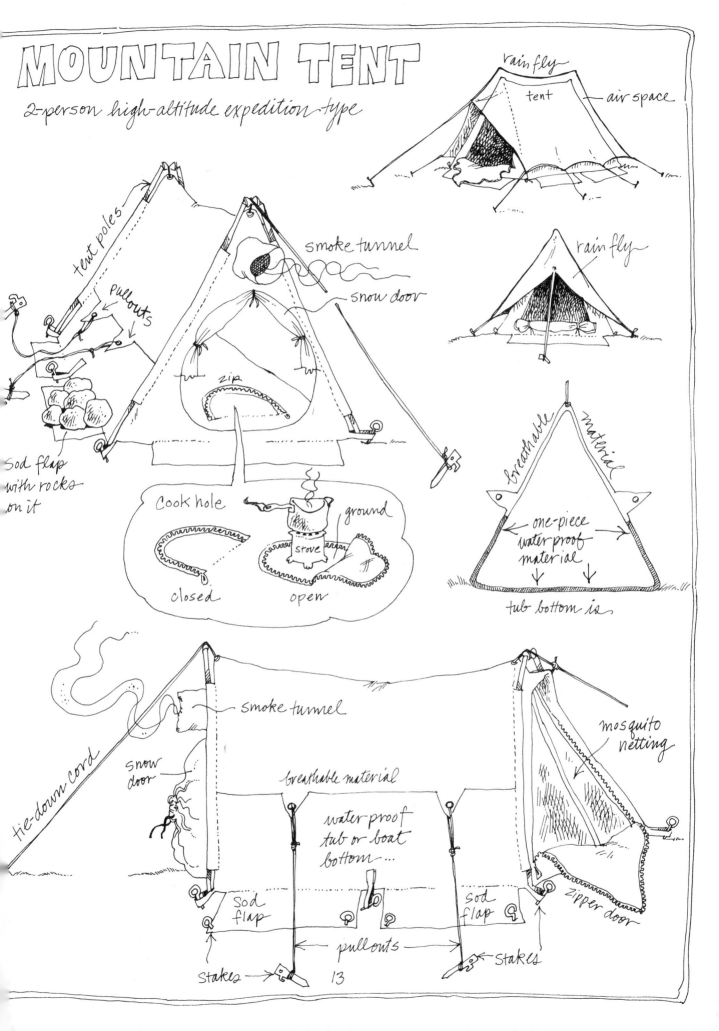

rainfly

tent

air space

tent poles

pullouts

smoke tunnel

snow door

zip

sod flap with rocks on it

Cook hole

ground

stove

closed

open

rain fly

breathable material

one-piece waterproof material

tub bottom is

smoke tunnel

tie-down cord

snow door

breathable material

water proof tub or boat bottom...

sod flap

sod flap

pullouts

mosquito netting

zipper door

stakes

stakes

13

VARIOUS TENTS

american indian tipi

family-size outside-frame-type tent...

regular

large

desert nomad tent

smaller outside-frame tent

dome tent

"prairie schooner" family tent

catenary-cut tent

McKinley tent with fly

water runs down rope, drips in tent

NO

(one-person tent)

no drips inside this way

Yes

tube tent (one-piece plastic)

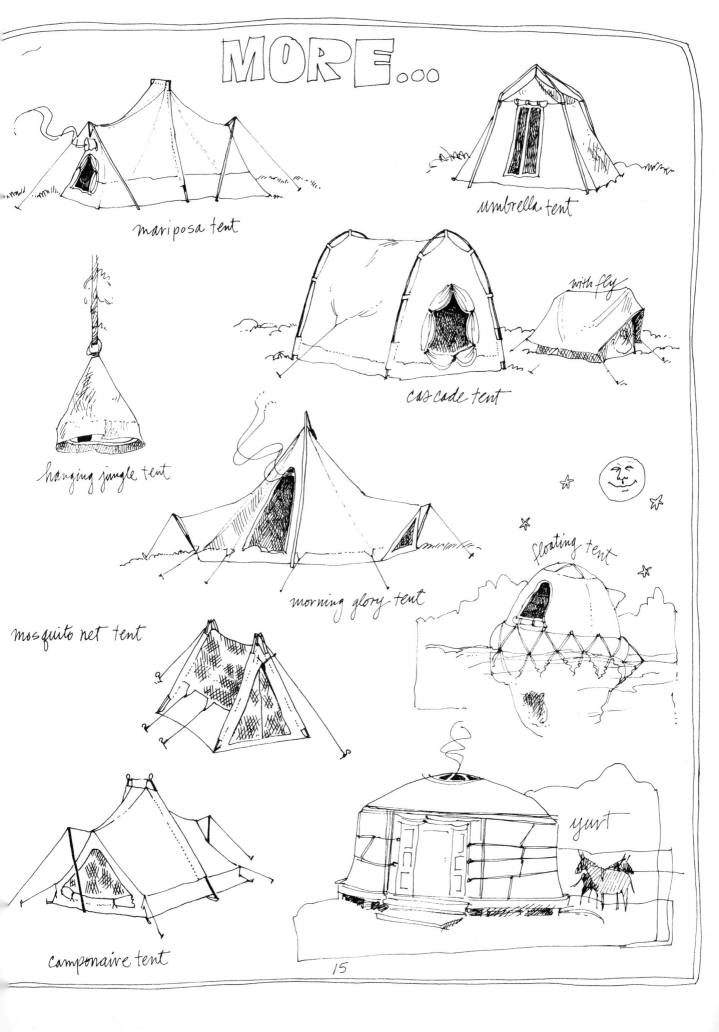

MORE...

mariposa tent

umbrella tent

cascade tent

with fly

hanging jungle tent

morning glory tent

floating tent

mosquito net tent

yurt

camponaire tent

15

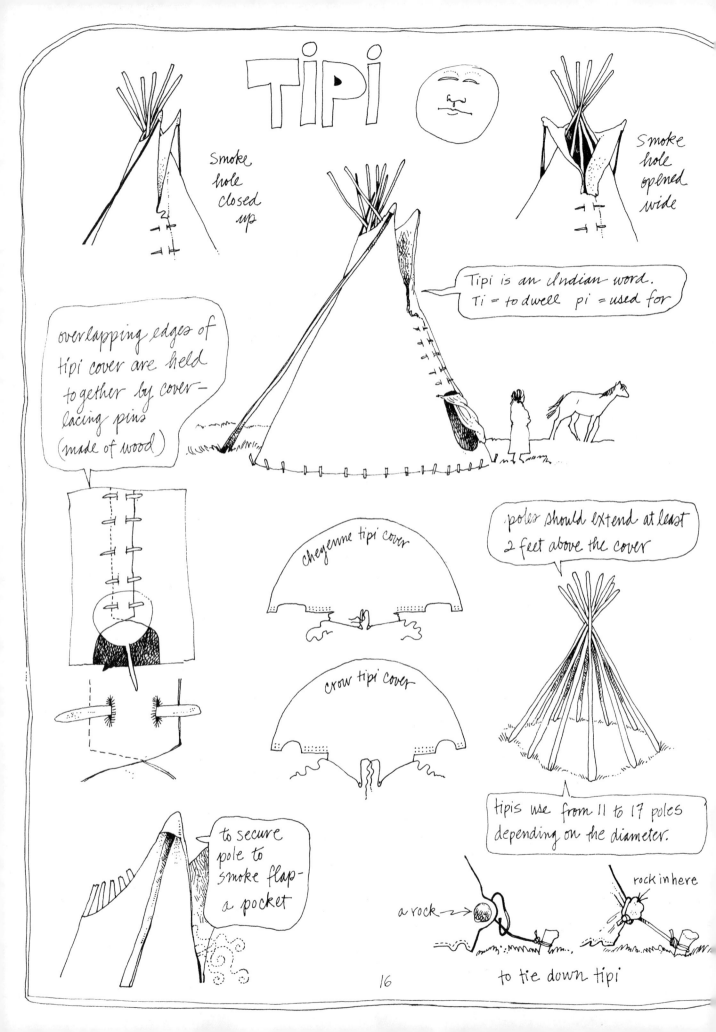

Tipi

smoke hole closed up

smoke hole opened wide

Tipi is an Indian word.
Ti = to dwell pi = used for

overlapping edges of tipi cover are held together by cover-lacing pins (made of wood)

cheyenne tipi cover

crow tipi cover

poles should extend at least 2 feet above the cover

tipis use from 11 to 17 poles depending on the diameter.

to secure pole to smoke flap - a pocket

a rock

rock in here

to tie down tipi

16

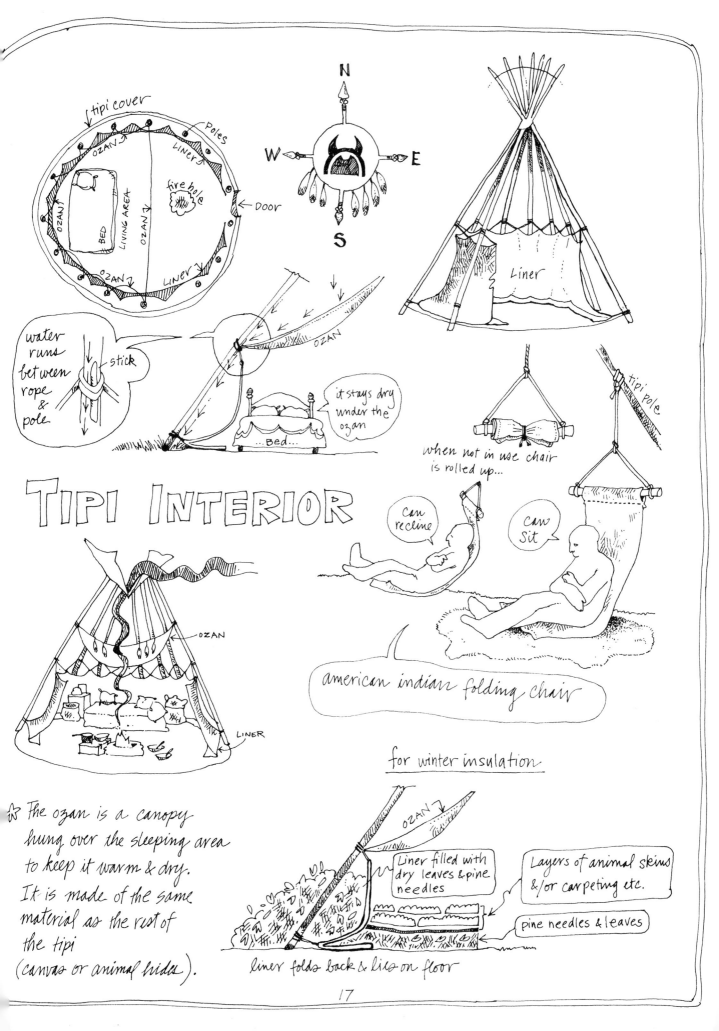

tipi cover

Poles

OZAN

OZAN

Liner

fire hole

BED

LIVING AREA

OZAN

← Door

OZAN

Liner

N

W

E

S

Liner

water runs between rope & pole

stick

it stays dry under the ozan

...Bed...

when not in use chair is rolled up...

tipi pole

can recline

can sit

american indian folding chair

TIPI INTERIOR

OZAN

LINER

for winter insulation

OZAN

Liner filled with dry leaves & pine needles

Layers of animal skins &/or carpeting etc.

pine needles & leaves

☆ The ozan is a canopy hung over the sleeping area to keep it warm & dry. It is made of the same material as the rest of the tipi (canvas or animal hides).

liner folds back & lies on floor

17

DESERT TENT

to support tent

tall

medium

short

9 POLES
3 sets of 3 poles, 3 different lengths

cover is a rectangular cloth

made of woven goat hair &/or sheeps' wool usually more than one cloth sewn together to make large one

oasis

tent

camels

people

dogs

sheep & goats

large wooden stakes... put at least 2 feet into sand

pole   deep in sand 1 foot or more

tops of poles should be rounded & smooth so as not to make holes in tent cover

when no stakes are available, people tie the rope to a bush & bury it in the sand

one open side
can also open both of these long sides

18

YURT

frame is covered with layers of wool material &/or canvas depending on the weather

North
West
East
Storage
bed
fire
Cook
Living Area
Storage
DOOR
South

supports for walls are expanding lattice made of wood ... like a kiddie gate

central compression ring

closed lattice

opened lattice

roof poles are tied to end of lattice poles then fit into holes in a central compression ring at top of yurt... this ring also serves as a smoke hole

frame is tied together

a yurt traditionally faces south so that the patch of sun light shining through the smoke hole acts as a clock

whole yurt can be carried by 1 or 2 camels

19

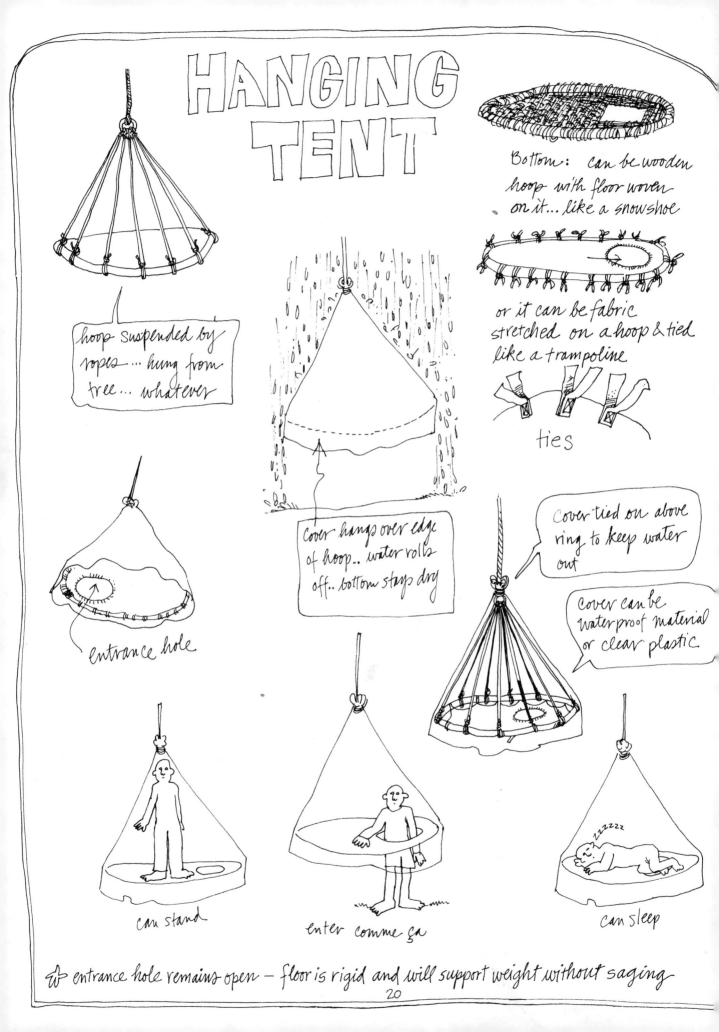

HANGING TENT

Bottom: can be wooden hoop with floor woven on it... like a snowshoe

or it can be fabric stretched on a hoop & tied like a trampoline

ties

hoop suspended by ropes ... hung from tree ... whatever

entrance hole

cover hangs over edge of hoop.. water rolls off.. bottom stays dry

cover tied on above ring to keep water out

cover can be waterproof material or clear plastic

can stand

enter comme ça

can sleep

⟳ entrance hole remains open — floor is rigid and will support weight without saging

20

HAMMOCK TENT

Strip of webbing sewn entire length of tent with loops at end for hanging

double-layer cloth outside, netting inside

bug net

net window

bug net here also

drawstrings on outside & inside

sleeping bag ↓

detail of hanging loops

can stand

can sit

Loops attached to ceiling for hanging clothes-line little hammocks as storage bins ✛

↑string   ↑bandana

anti-bug net

one side closed can be used as storage area

can open one end or both

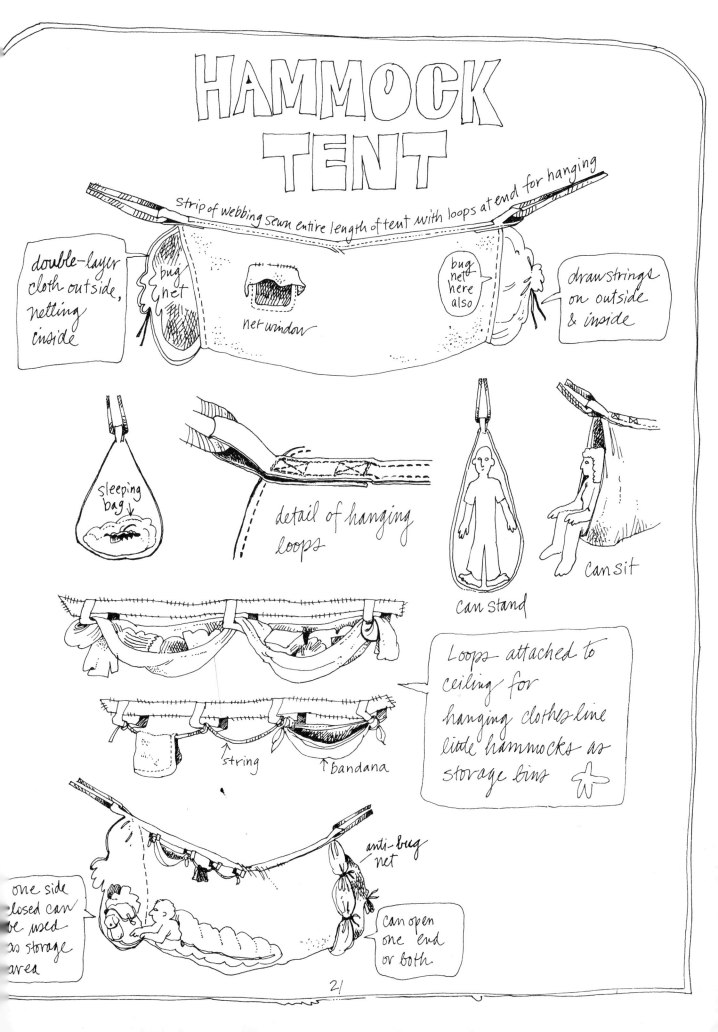

PORTABLE UMBRELLA TENT

overlapping door

tent open

tent closed

clear panels

air flows in & out - but not water

umbrella ribs

hooks

grommets

wall of tent hangs from umbrella

sleeping person

overhang keeps you dry

Zipper door

zip

stake

bottom sewn in

stake

FLOATING TENT

giant-truck inner tube for the base of tent...

to support tent

fiber-glass ribs

← or air ribs

tent floor & top made of waterproof material

Loops or flaps with grommets for tying tent down

transparent top — made of heavy vinyl

air vent

zipper door

Screen window zips shut on the inside

window from inside

can be sewn on

ready made air vent from a marine supply house

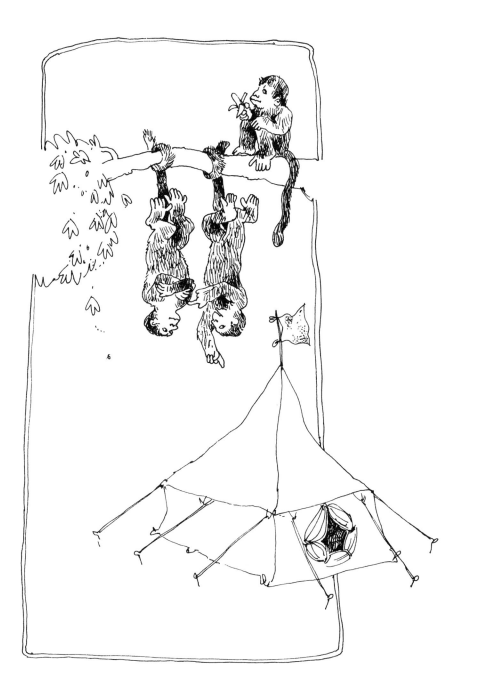

LOOK AT IT THIS WAY

When you're in your house and it starts to rain, you close the windows . . . but you don't close *all* the windows, just the ones on the side where the rain is coming in. Think about it in a tent. You don't have windows, you have flaps or flies.

On most tents the flaps are too small, and don't work in a partially-open position. In addition, the window is usually in the center of a wall, under tension, and therefore slightly concave. The result is that the water runs directly toward the flaps.

If you're going to have flaps on your tent, make sure that they're much larger than the window, otherwise you're going to have a constant rain problem. If you can, install a pullout under the window, or near it, so that area will be out of the normal rain-drainage route.

Good rain flaps are important. If you can close them on the side of your tent that the rain is coming from, you can leave the other side open, and eliminate condensation and moisture. The same applies for the front door: it must have rain flaps that will keep rain out, yet allow air to come in. There's no reason to close all your windows just because it's raining.

LOOKING

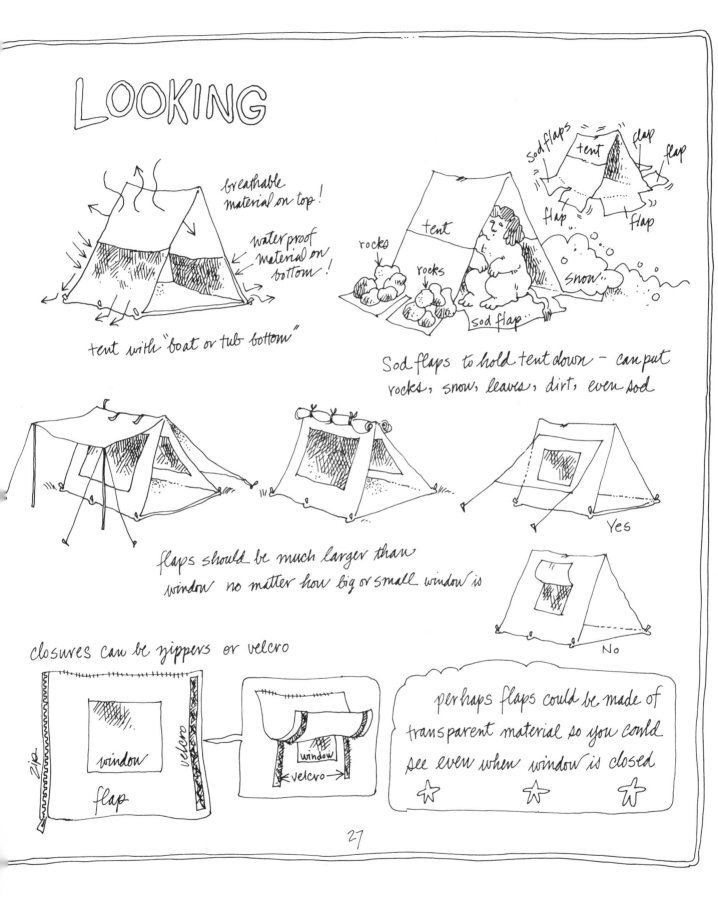

breathable material on top!

waterproof material on bottom!

tent with "boat or tub bottom"

sod flaps
tent
flap
flap
flap
flap

rocks
tent
rocks
snow
sod flap

Sod flaps to hold tent down — can put rocks, snow, leaves, dirt, even sod

flaps should be much larger than window no matter how big or small window is

Yes

No

closures can be zippers or velcro

zip
window
velcro
flap

window
velcro

perhaps flaps could be made of transparent material so you could see even when window is closed
☆ ☆ ✩

27

"anyone who buys a tent with a pole in the middle of the doorway deserves to walk into it."

If you were building a house, you would never put an obstruction in the middle of the doorway. So don't build or buy a tent with a pole in the entrance way.

Another archaic and unsuitable form of tent design is the locating of poles in the center of the tent. Someone will inevitably roll against it in the middle of the night and knock it out, and then the whole tent will come down.

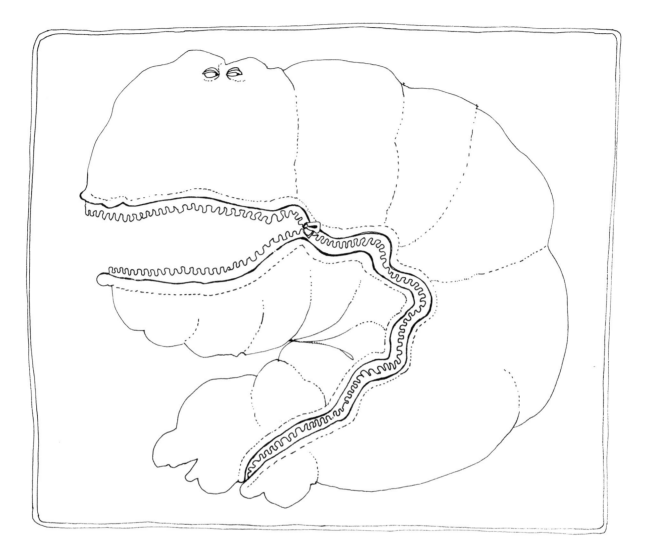

ZIPPERS

Metal zippers are totally out of harmony with the kind of environment they have to live in. Not only can a metal zipper attract lightning but it can also rust, and its corrosion produces a chemical reaction which rots out the canvas where the teeth are embedded. A much better alternative are zippers made of plastic material. Look for tents that use the large-toothed, double-slider type.

Tents that are going to be used in sand or snow have little sod flaps around their bottoms. These flaps are spread out, and sand, earth, snow, or rocks are placed on top of them. When these areas are weighted down they take some of the strain off the stakes and make the tent impermeable to wind.

People have the false notion that they have to dig a trench around their tent. They think that this will make the water flow off in another direction. If you're on flat ground, digging a trench does nothing. If you're on high or sloped ground and you're going to depend on a trench to rechannel the water, forget it. Look for a new tent site. Some tents have a "boat bottom," a waterproof floor that comes a few inches up the sides. If the water flows in the direction of your tent, it will flow under it, or around it, but it definitely won't be absorbed by the bottom.

Most tents are made of either plastic, nylon, cotton, vinyl, rubberized combinations, or waxed or unwaxed combinations of all of the above.

The Siberians, Mongolians, and the Bedouins used wool of either the yak, sheep, or goat to make their tents.

As Australia is the world's largest producer of wool, I wrote to their testing bureau and asked about woolen tents. Strangely enough, they had done no research on them.

Silk is a strong and natural material. I met a European camper once who had a tent that was made back in the thirties completely of silk. It had faded from years of sunlight, wind, and rain pounding on it, but the tent was in remarkably good condition. It was a large tent, big enough to stand in, and was built to be tied to trees and stakes. Unfortunately, at present, there are no commercially-made silk tents.

Jason McWhorter (an artist who has done several of the drawings in "soft house visions") owned a tent for a number of years. He painted designs on the roof and walls.

All of his paintings are still clear after many years, although the basic color of the tent has faded. He used acrylic paints, and they maintained their brightness. His was a cotton canvas tent; but I'm not sure how well this would work on the nylon varieties.

If you want to experiment, buy a piece of potential tent-material and use that for your experimentation. Try several wash-and-dry cycles to see how it holds up.

It's possible that some of the chemicals in paint might disintegrate the synthetic fabric or coatings. It's also feasible that the paint won't adhere to a waxed, coated fabric.

TENT DESIGN

(*materials for construction of camping equipment*)

If you get the desire to design and execute items for your camping experiences, here's a bit of advice. Natural materials work best with natural materials. Synthetic should be mated with synthetic.

For example . . .

Wool material sewn with polyester thread . . . bad!
Nylon material sewn with cotton . . . bad!
Cotton material sewn with linen . . . good!
Polyester material sewn with polyester thread . . . good!

Zippers are a way to close an open space easily. Lately, plastic zippers have taken over the outdoor market.

There is one type of zipper called the *coil*. This kind can be zipped around curves much better than a normal toothed zipper. If, however, the zip is just a long straight run, a large-toothed zipper will provide the most strength and durability.

Zippers are usually sewn in, and whenever there's a sewn joint, there are needle holes. Each one of these holes is a potential place for a leak, so design your zipper areas to exhibit natural rain-shedding abilities. Zippers cannot be made water-proof, but the area around them can.

All zippers should be *double sliders*. This means that they can be opened from either end, so you can control ventilation. If you do this with tent flaps and doorways, some part of the tent can always be left open to allow an air flow. This helps minimize condensation during rain.

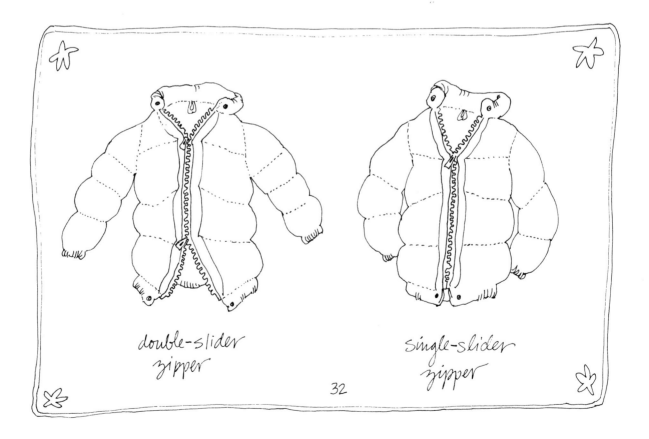

double-slider
zipper

single-slider
zipper

FOR ZIPPERS

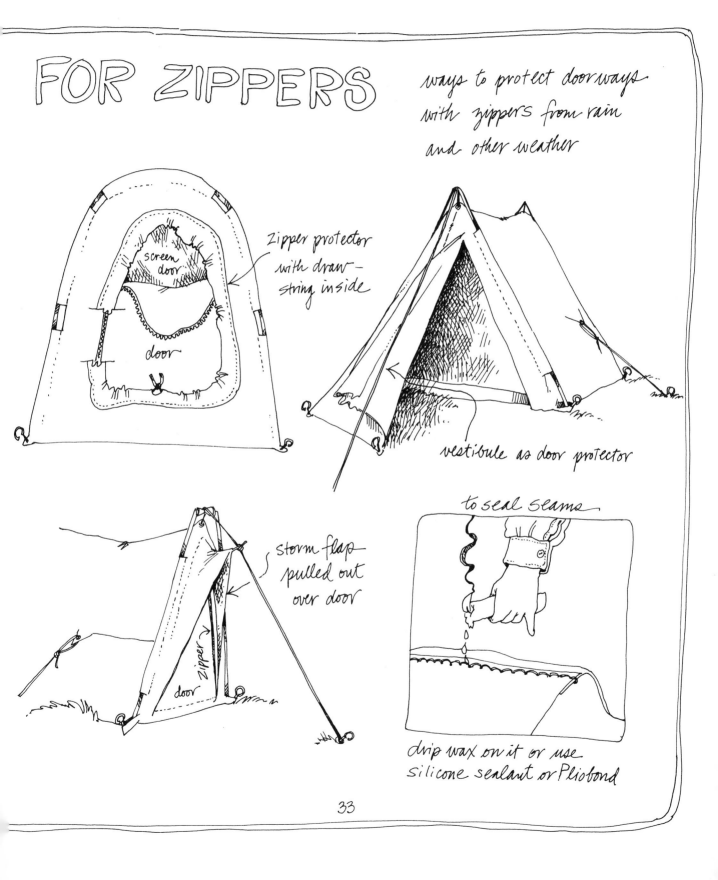

ways to protect doorways with zippers from rain and other weather

Zipper protector with draw-string inside

screen door

door

vestibule as door protector

storm flap pulled out over door

door zippers

to seal seams

drip wax on it or use silicone sealant or Pliobond

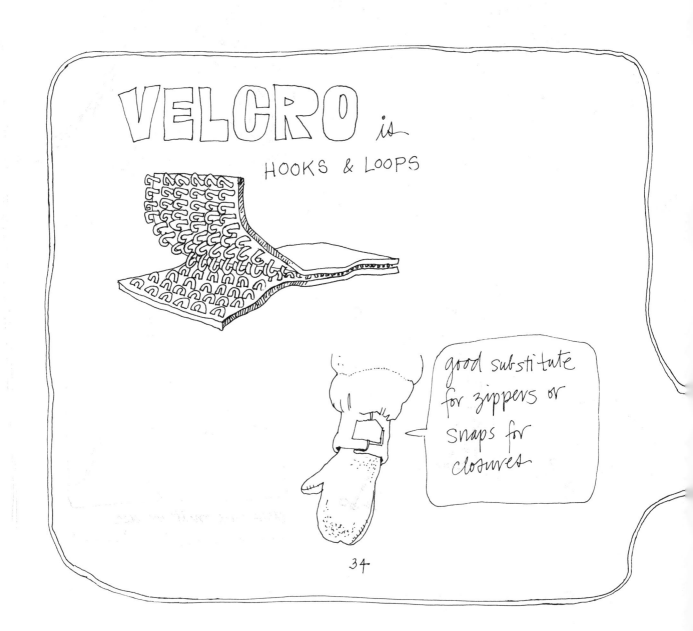

VELCRO is

HOOKS & LOOPS

good substitute
for zippers or
snaps for
closures

34

Zippers can be really hard to undo. Sometimes it takes both hands to unzip them, either because they're under tension or because something inherent in their design makes it difficult.

Nina Miller told me of a tent experience that she'd had at a newly-opened tent and camping store.

A friend of hers was going to the Yucatan, in Mexico, to camp, so they went to the store to find a pack and some camping equipment. There were tents set up, and she got in one, and her friend zipped it up. When she tried to unzip herself, she couldn't, because the zipper had stuck. As hard as they tried, neither she nor her friend could unzip it. Meanwhile all the sales people were running around the store and were too busy to help her. Luckily the tent had a cook hole (an opening in the floor which usually unzips and exposes the ground underneath, so you can use a cook stove in that area without burning the material around it).

She unzipped the cook hole, and a bunch of people held the tent in the air so she could crawl out.

Try out all zippers, fastenings, and tie-downs in your tent before you take it out in the woods. If there are any problems, it will be much better to find them out at home.

I think a zipper should be designed so you can just run right through it if you have to. It should be constructed so the netting on the door won't tear—and it should be immediately self-repairing.

I put this idea to the YKK zipper people, the largest manufacturers of zippers in the world, and their reply was simply that they'd done no research on it.

BUYING A TENT

As the day I was going to be living in a tent drew near, I started to go through all the newspapers, outdoor magazines, and sportsmen's catalogues I could find. I found that nearly every imaginable size and form of tent is available.

After much perusal, I went to a department-store sale, and bought a 9' x 12' outside-frame tent. It was a waxed-cotton-canvas tent, with a cotton sewn-in floor, two windows (one on each side) with rain flaps, a mosquito-netting door—and a big mistake, as it leaked all over and the floor rotted in the spring rain.

A catalogue will give the basic structure and color of a tent, but you shouldn't buy one without first going to a store and thoroughly examining it. Camping and tenting stores are really adult toy stores. You should be allowed to feel, play with, and see how everything works, before you buy it. You wouldn't buy a pair of shoes without first trying them on, nor would you buy a car without test-driving it. See and touch what you're planning to get, whether it's a sleeping bag, pack, cook stove or tent, and then decide if it's really what you want.

If you or a group of people are going to be spending an extended period of time in a tent, you should get the largest one you can carry and afford. This way each person can have a reasonable amount of privacy, and enough room to lean back and relax, without getting in each other's way.

CHOOSING THE SITE

Your choice of tent location is one of the most important aspects of the tent experience. Sanitation, safety, growing things, drainage, storm security are all dependent on it. Don't let aesthetics trick you. It's wiser to find a suitable location rather than one which is just pretty.

Before you get your tent set up, walk around the area in your bare feet and feel for any sharp projections. If you find any, try to remove them. If there are sharp objects boring into your tent, they will wear it out quickly, and be uncomfortable to sit or roll over on.

If the projection under your tent happens to be the root of a tree, I suggest that you move the tent. Put your tent up in accordance with the local terrain and surroundings.

Boulders are like icebergs. You might see a little thing sticking out of the ground and think, "Oh, I'll just dig it out and backfill it with dirt," but you just could be looking at the tip of a 10-ton boulder.

Check the area for dead trees or trees with dead limbs. If a tree is standing dead and a high wind comes, there's a chance that a branch will fall off. If it comes down in your direction, from 50 to 60 feet above, it will go right through your tent. Try to pick an area where the trees are young and healthy. Older trees usually have some dead limbs. In the summertime, when the limbs are green, the dead ones are easy to pick out, but in the fall or the wintertime it's difficult to sort the dead from the living. If the branches are devoid of bark, have peeling bark, or are split, I'd pick another place to camp.

If you camp near a lake or stream, be at least 150 feet away for sanitation purposes and for reason of the waterborne bug population.

If you're in a place where strong winds are coming predominately from one direction, try to get trees, small hills, rock piles, bushes, shrubs, or *anything* between you and the wind.

For the purpose of drainage, try for ground that is slightly sloped and open. Eroded areas usually indicate a high water runoff, and they are very bad places to pitch your tent.

The Bedouins, who depend on water holes for their life and for the life of their animals (which is what their wealth system is based on), rarely camp in an oasis. They can't afford to take the chance of animals urinating or defecating in the area and having it poison their water system. They usually camp at least a half-mile from an oasis.

Make sure that your latrine isn't up-country from your tent site. When a good rain comes, the ground will overflow, and water will start to run off in your direction. The result will be most unpleasant.

There are a variety of state or privately-owned campsites where every 100 feet or so there will be a tent and a campfire area. These are renting from $1.00 to $4.50 a day. If you enjoy the close proximity of voices and other people and still want a tenting experience, you'll find this a good way to go. You will be able to hear the crickets at night, and the wood sounds will start to come on, but you will be in a highly-populated area for its relative size.

About a year ago, as I was sitting in my tent in the afternoon, the sky suddenly got very dark. I looked for clouds but couldn't see any.

The next thing I knew, branches and trees were being flung around overhead. The wind was tremendously high, and because of a vacuum around my tent, it expanded like a balloon. In 30 seconds this phenomenon had passed, and the sky was bright again. I climbed to the top of a hill and looked down the valley. I saw a huge slot in the forest where nothing was standing. Trees were uprooted and tossed in every direction. In a half a minute, a tornado had come and gone.

I went to survey the damage, and found that a truckstop about three-quarters of a mile away had been totally destroyed; trailer trucks had been thrown into the trees. People had been

the tornado of '73

killed. Yet my tent, which was almost directly in the path of the tornado, was undamaged.

The reason is that I was camping in a slight ravine where the top of the tent was still ten or twelve feet below the peak of the hills on both sides. Therefore, the tornado winds blew by me. Camping in a ravine, however, is not always a good idea, as they are susceptible, in some areas, to mid-summer flash floods. I picked the spot because the ground was flat, and there was a good view. Lucky for me.

If you know what area you're going to be camping in, try to obtain a topographical map. It will tell you the general elevations and show you where the water runoffs are. (If you get lost in the woods, an old survival trick is to walk downhill until you hit a stream runoff area. If you follow it downstream long enough, you'll come to a town.) By using a topographical map, you can pick spots that will have high appeal in terms of view, practicality, and comfort before you get to the area.

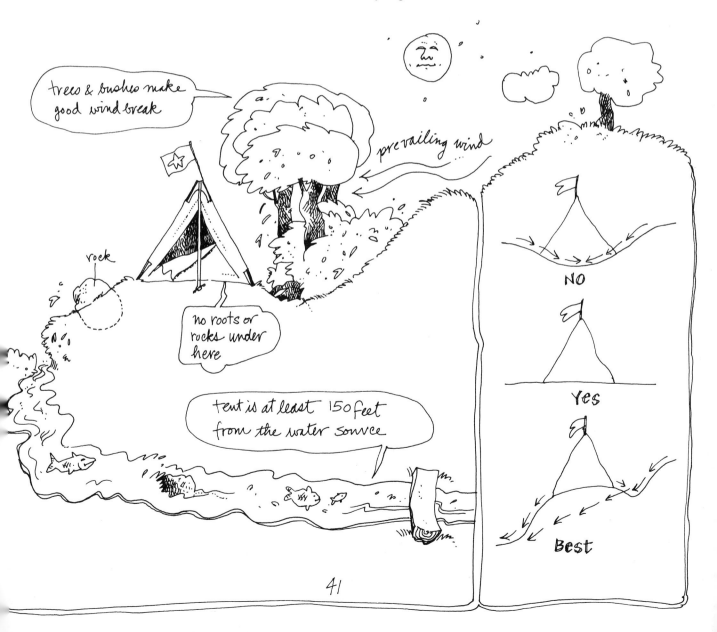

trees & bushes make good wind break

prevailing wind

rock

no roots or rocks under here

tent is at least 150 feet from the water source

NO

Yes

Best

PUTTING UP YOUR TENT

After you've lived in a house for a while, you can walk into it even when it's pitch black and know exactly where everything is. If you familiarize yourself with your tent by erecting it where you live, and examining it before you take it into the woods, you will begin to get a feeling for where the zipper, poles, and flaps are.

Here is one method for erecting a tent. If your tent has a nonwaterproof floor in it, place a plastic vapor barrier on the ground in the area where you want your tent put up. Then set up your frame.

With all the windows and doors zipped closed, stretch the bottom part out to its stakes or poles. It's important that all the zippers, doors, and windows be closed while you're setting up your tent—otherwise there might not be enough slack to close them when the tent is fully raised.

When you've done that, take a knife and slice away all the excess plastic, leaving a piece the exact size of your tent.

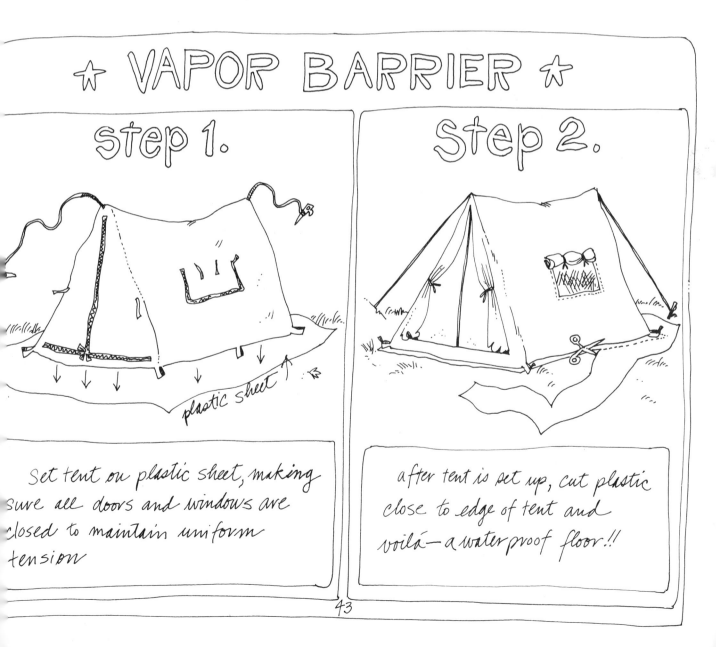

☆ VAPOR BARRIER ☆

step 1.

plastic sheet

Set tent on plastic sheet, making sure all doors and windows are closed to maintain uniform tension

step 2.

after tent is set up, cut plastic close to edge of tent and voilà—a waterproof floor!!

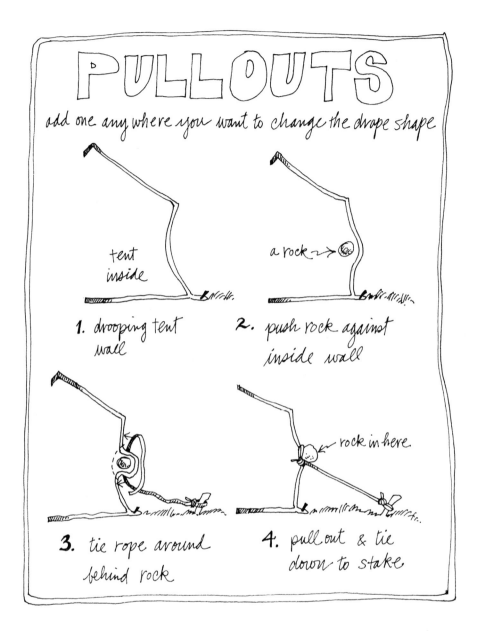

PULLOUTS

add one anywhere you want to change the drape shape

tent
inside

1. drooping tent wall

a rock →

2. push rock against inside wall

3. tie rope around behind rock

rock in here

4. pull out & tie down to stake

Next, hook the rest of your tent to its poles. Get a general look at it, and if it sags anyplace where it shouldn't, remove the sag. The best way to do this is either to stretch it to a different spot or to change the angle of the pole. You could also add a pullout in that area. A pullout can consist of a rock on the inside of the tent, pushed out hard enough so that you can put a loop of rope around it and hook it to an available stake or pole. In addition to giving you extra room inside, it makes the tent walls drain better.

Most people are used to dealing with flame in a closed place, a fireplace or a steel stove. There doesn't have to be much thought about wind direction or sparks because there are doors that can be closed. When you deal with an open campfire, or an open fire inside your tent, it's very *un*contained.

The material manufacturers I spoke with were very concerned with the fire problem. A child had been critically burned in a tent, and suddenly the industry was deluged with demands for fireproof tents.

There are companies now offering every tent they have with fireproofing as an option, at no extra charge, because as yet it's not mandatory.

Nylon is a more recent material than cotton, and as a result the cotton manufacturers have been fireproofing their products for a much longer period of time.

CPAI 84 is a tent-industry standard for measuring the susceptibility of fabrics to open flame. Under a standardized condition, sample fabric is tested by being exposed to an open flame for 12 seconds, and the length of the burn is measured. To meet the standard, the fabric must not allow the burn to exceed more than 10 inches, and should be substantially below that. The fabric must also be self-extinguishing within 2 seconds after removal of the flame. The CPAI standard has necessitated the use of heavier coatings to preserve the lifetime fire retardancy of lighter fabrics.

Fireproofing tents doesn't negate the fact that the forest and animal life around you aren't fireproofed, so exercise caution with flame.

You can go 50 feet off a highway in rural America and no one will ever see your tent site if it's chosen well. The thing that will be visible is fire, or smoke.

A group of friends went to the top of a mountain to stay the night, cook some dinner, and generally have a good time.

After a while, lights started coming out of the sky. Suddenly they heard voice-noises coming from behind them over loud-speakers. They looked down the mountain and saw lights coming up at them.

A ranger, sitting in his fire station about four mountain ranges away, had seen the orange glow from their campfire and assumed that there was a forest fire—so he turned in the alarm.

My friends were given severe verbal lashings from the local police, the local ambulance companies, and everyone else who got pulled out of bed at two in the morning.

I've found that forest rangers and fire watchers in the back country really feel a close attachment to the forest. To them it's more than a job. They're really quite friendly and will tell you where fresh water can be found, help you with maps or in any way they can. They just have to be convinced that you're traveling in harmony with what they're trying to protect.

EATING, HEATING,
& LIGHTING

There are two basic uses for a stove. One is to heat something local to the flame, like a pot, and the other is to heat a large space.

There are many modern, compact stoves on the market. They weigh about a pound, are made of spun aluminum and brass, and fold up into neat packages.

For cooking, I suggest that you use canned Sterno. Sterno costs less than any other comparable fuel, is easy to use, and can be bought in any supermarket. All you do to operate Sterno is take off the lid and put a match to it. To put it out, just slide the lid over the top. Even if you leave it out in cold or rainy weather, it can still be lit instantaneously.

Hexamine tablets are an emergency fuel that will help you start a fire under less-than-ideal conditions. Individually, they weigh 1 ounce, and burn with a red-hot flame for about 12 minutes.

For cooking and eating utensils, the only materials I would suggest using are glass, ceramics, stainless steel, or cast iron. Aluminum corrodes, and little white spots of aluminum salts appear—they are harmful for your stomach. Also, certain foods will react with aluminum and cause a chemical change that is not beneficial to your body. You can use aluminum cookware if it is coated with Teflon. This way, in effect, you're cooking on Teflon while taking advantage of aluminum's light carrying weight.

A small carbide light can serve as a good easy-to-store-and-carry reading lamp. This type of light burns acetylene gas, produced by mixing carbide dust with water. It is a very safe and intensely brilliant light. The fuel is fairly inexpensive, and one filling burns for a long time. The carbide light requires no pumping or priming, and has a built in self-igniter, like the wheel on a cigarette lighter.

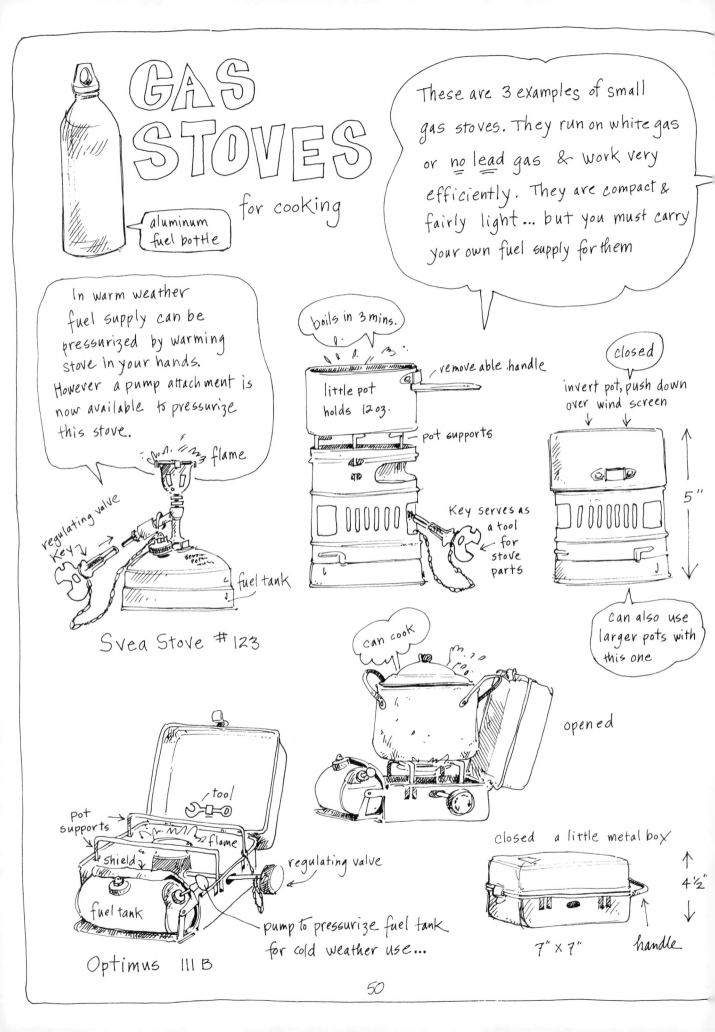

GAS STOVES
for cooking

aluminum fuel bottle

These are 3 examples of small gas stoves. They run on white gas or no lead gas & work very efficiently. They are compact & fairly light... but you must carry your own fuel supply for them

In warm weather fuel supply can be pressurized by warming stove in your hands. However a pump attachment is now available to pressurize this stove.

flame

regulating valve
Key

fuel tank

Svea Stove #123

boils in 3 mins.

little pot holds 12 oz.

remove able handle

pot supports

Key serves as a tool for stove parts

closed

invert pot, push down over wind screen

5"

can also use larger pots with this one

can cook

opened

tool

Pot supports

flame

shield

regulating valve

fuel tank

pump to pressurize fuel tank for cold weather use...

Optimus III B

closed   a little metal box

4½"

7" × 7"   handle

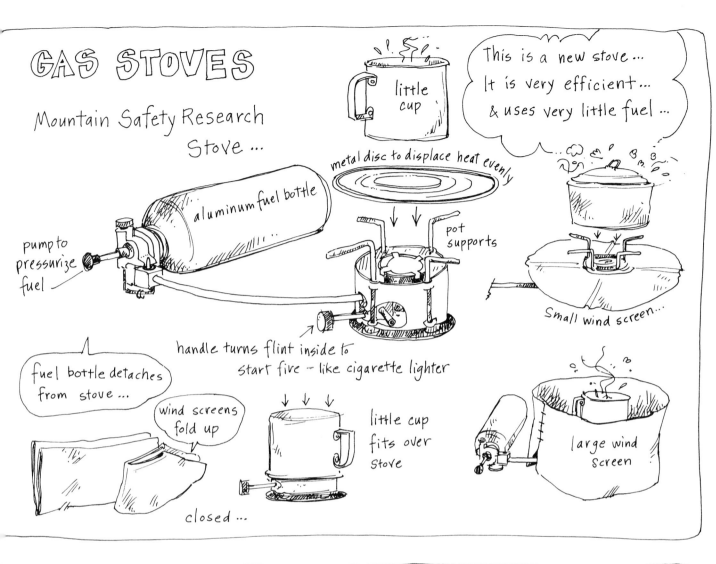

One of the safest units used to heat a tent is a catalytic cold-flame heater. Even if it falls over, it won't burn anything, and it doesn't consume much oxygen. Catalytic heaters run on bottle or liquid gas. The only drawback with this type of heater is its weight. Unless you will be staying in one place for a long period of time, it is impractical to carry one with you.

An interesting dual tool is a kerosene heater and cooker. It looks like a column. When the bottom is lit, it becomes a heater. Further up, it resembles a burner from a gas range, and that part is usable as a single burner. Kerosene uses up the oxygen in the air, and gives off carbon monoxide, so make sure that when you use it, you have suitable ventilation.

Sterno

put cooking
pot on
here

TOMATO

fire

tin can for stove
leave bottom in

can heat pot here

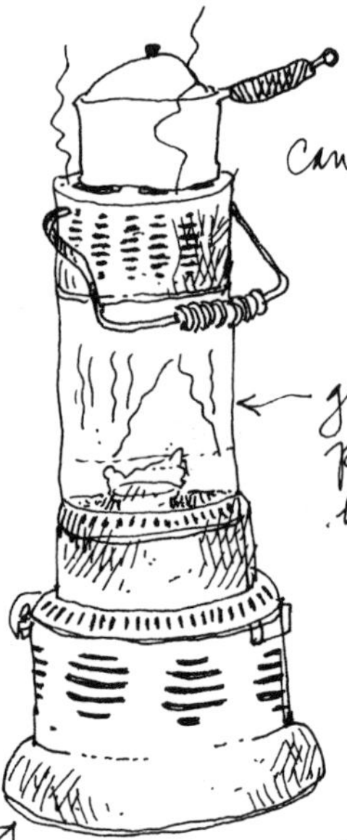

glass
provides
heat & light

kerosene heater &
cooker

grate for cooking

mantle for burning
flame

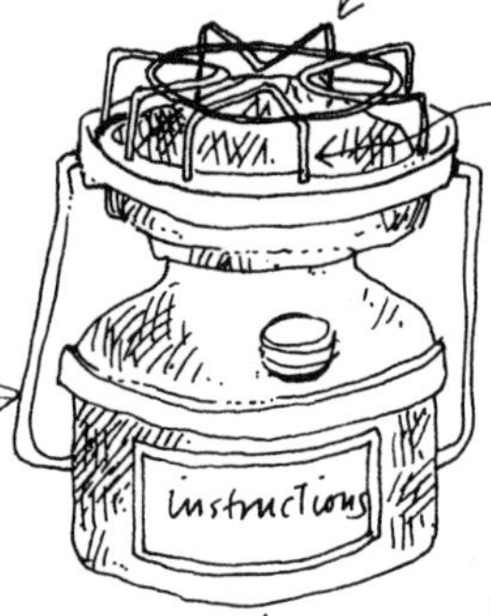

handle

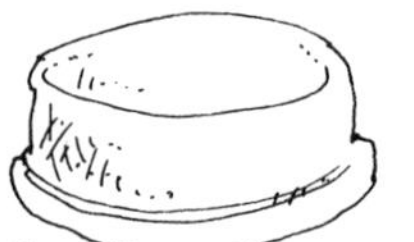

instructions

lid to cover when
carrying

catalytic cold flame heater

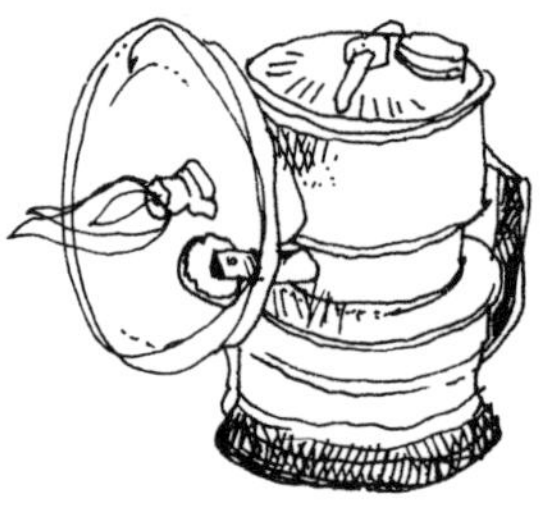

carbide light

STOVES
& STUFF ★

Hexamine tablet

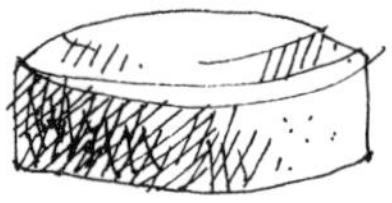

burns for
12 minutes

will boil a
cup of water →

can for stove → tuna

52

A POLOG

from Siberia

a yurt

can open all sides

poles

Bed

cloth covers

piece of moss
for a wick

oil

wooden bowl

heat & lamp for polog

a polog is like a small tent within a tent. it is built around the bed... this gives added protection from the cold within the yurt... people would take their own heat & light supply into the polog...

☆ The lamp is usually placed beside the bed. However, an open flame in any tent requires extreme caution.

FOOD

You can grow your own food, but while you're waiting for it you'll probably have to make trips to the nearest grocery store. When you buy food, deal mainly with dried or fresh, rather than frozen, foods—unless you're winter camping.

Things I buy at the market are figs, powdered milk, dates, honey, raisins, cheese, peanut butter, olives, nuts, fruits, and vegetables. I buy the fruit as green as possible so it will ripen over a longer period of time.

If you like cereal in the morning, there are some good natural ones available in local supermarkets that, either cooked or uncooked, make a good meal.

If you buy food that comes in paper packages, I suggest that you transfer them to plastic bags or containers. Paper deteriorates with moisture, and therefore the contents are susceptible to spoilage.

Don't put fresh fruits and vegetables in jars, because unless they can breathe, they will rot quickly.

Premixed juices will last longer if they're unopened and not left out in the sun. Once they're opened, they'll last only a couple of hours.

If you happen to be near water and want to go fishing (line and twig work as well as anything else), you can supplement your diet and stretch your food supply. Ancient mariners salted down beef and pork, and it kept well without freezing. Fish can be salted, hung up to dry in the sun, and kept unrefrigerated for six months.

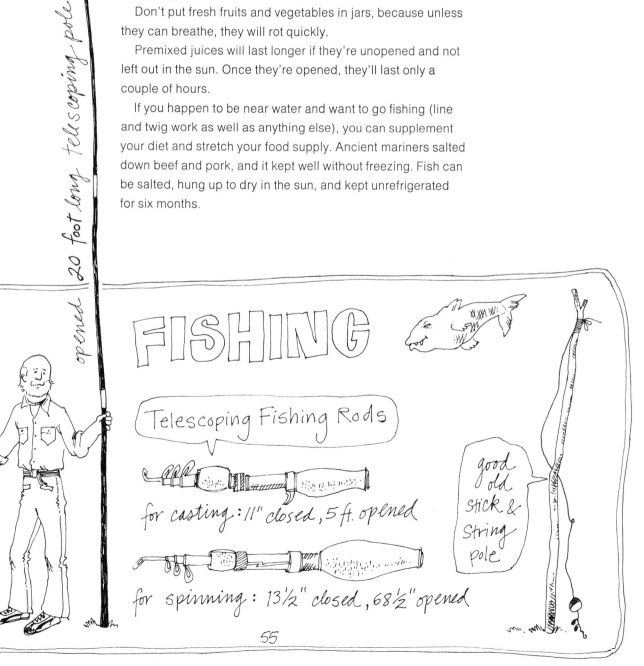

opened 20 foot long telescoping pole

Closed 52½"

FISHING

Telescoping Fishing Rods

for casting: 11" closed, 5 ft. opened

for spinning: 13½" closed, 68½" opened

good old stick & string pole

FOOD

Stuff sack should be of breathable material

stuff sack

with food inside hung from tree

Safe from varments

LISTER BAG

white canvas water proof— holds 36 gals.

hang in shade for cool water— in sun for warm water

Spigots

jar of fermenting apple juice with balloon

RAISINS granola p'nuts sugar flour

transfer foods from paper containers to plastic ones

polyethylene canteen... no dent...no rust...

Unpasteurized apple juice doesn't keep well, but if it starts to spoil, don't despair. Take a couple handfuls of sugar or a box of raisins and a package of activated yeast, and dump it in the jug. Then put a big balloon over the top of the jug. Store it in a warm, shady place, and after about 21 days, take the balloon off and give it a try.

I bought 2 loaves of bread to do an experiment with. One was a loaf of all-natural grain with no preservatives, and the other was a loaf of popular white bread loaded with preservatives. I stored them side by side, about an inch apart, on the same shelf, facing the same direction, under a tree by the tent site.

After 5 days the loaf *with* all the "preservatives" showed some green mold. I opened the other loaf of bread and parted all the slices: there wasn't the slightest sign of mold anywhere.

It's a good idea to store all your food, but especially fresh items, in a wooden box or a bag which hangs from a tree. The box or bag should be able to breathe, and not be air- or water-tight. It will also benefit the food if it is kept in a cool, shady place.

Mushroom books and other foraging books are very nice to have along. If you want to get one to help you, make sure it depicts the plant. In addition, find someone who knows the forest and can relate both book and picture to the real article.

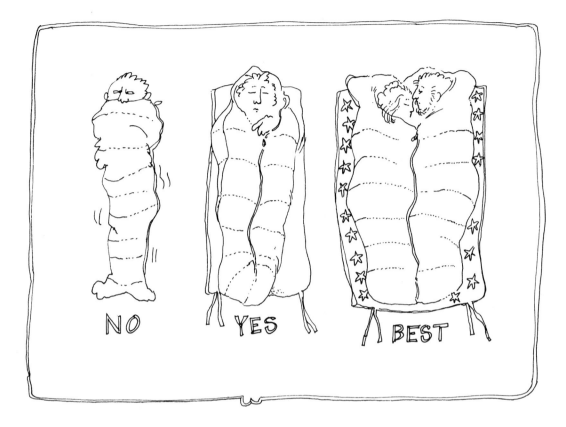

NO   YES   BEST

Invest in a ⅜"–½"-thick closed-cell foam pad to put underneath your sleeping bag. This type of mattress won't absorb water. If the sleeping bag you have, or intend to buy, has the bottom part of it made from foam, you won't have to carry a separate pad.

FOAM sleeping bag

(will work from 65° to 0° F)

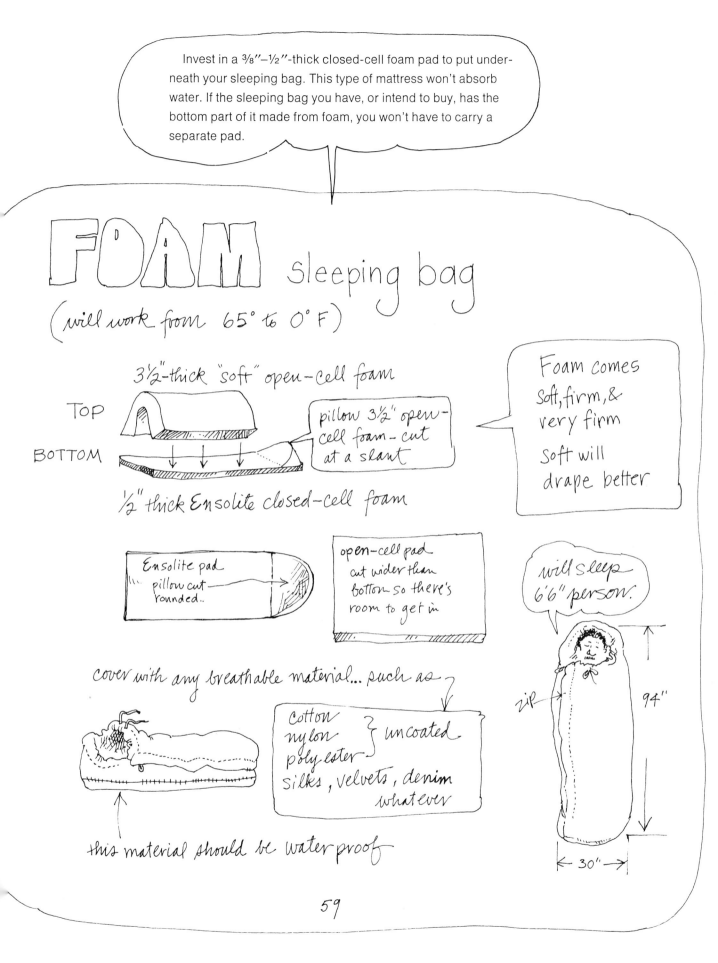

3½"-thick "soft" open-cell foam

TOP

BOTTOM

pillow 3½" open-cell foam – cut at a slant

½" thick Ensolite closed-cell foam

Foam comes soft, firm, & very firm

Soft will drape better

Ensolite pad pillow cut rounded..

open-cell pad cut wider than bottom so there's room to get in

will sleep 6'6" person.

cover with any breathable material... such as

cotton
nylon   } uncoated
polyester
silks, velvets, denim
                whatever

zip→

94"

←— 30" —→

this material should be waterproof

sleeping bags

sleeping bag being aired out

food bag

plastic tent

A sleeping bag is designed to keep you warm, not to fit like a straightjacket, and if that's how it feels, don't buy it.

Incidentally, in the winter, if you breathe within your sleeping bag, it won't keep you warm. Your breath only adds to the moisture level, and its vapor acts as a conductor for the cold.

A sleeping bag is a very personal thing. It's going to be your traveling cocoon; therefore, if you make the right choice of materials, there should be no such thing as an uncomfortable night.

A sleeping bag accumulates moisture inside from your body. If you leave it covered up during the day, you're not giving it a chance to air out and sanitize itself.

I make a practice, every day the sun shines, to pull out my sleeping bag, shake it, turn it inside out, and hang it over a rope in the sun. Take your bedroll and foam pad out once or twice a week and hang them in the sun. That is the best way to rid your bedroll of any dank or musty odors.

There are three highly acceptable kinds of fill used in the manufacturing of sleeping bags: down, polyester, and foam.

Down is the warmest for its weight, but it absorbs moisture and is totally useless when wet.

Polyester weighs more and doesn't compress as well as down, but it retains less than 1% moisture, and therefore makes an excellent insulation material in wet climates.

A combination of open- and closed-cell foam can be custom formulated to exhibit characteristics of permeability, compress-ability, and shaping. A foam sleeping bag is an excellent idea which, at this point, has not received very much attention from major manufacturers.

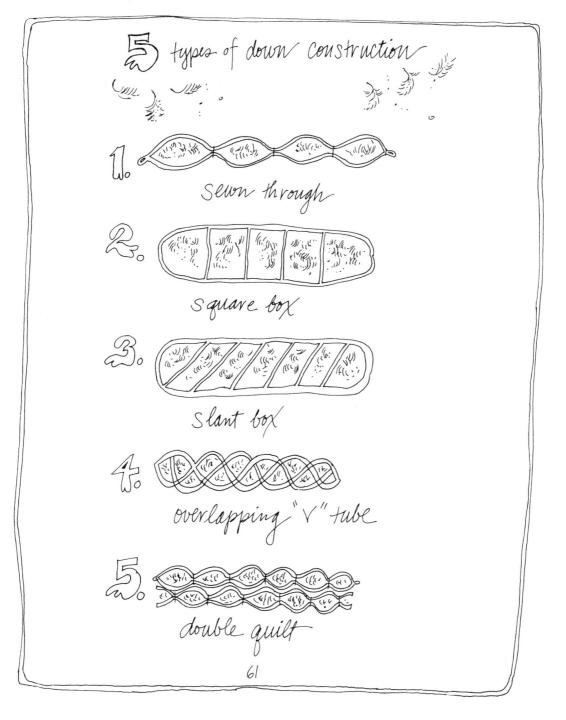

5 types of down construction

1. sewn through

2. square box

3. slant box

4. overlapping "v" tube

5. double quilt

HAMMOCKS

nylon net hammock

On a sunny day, the most relaxing thing I can think of is to get in a hammock and hang. A hammock can also be a nice way to spend part of an evening. In the morning and during the day you see all the birds, and how the clouds play through the tops of the trees. At night the stars come out and the atmosphere changes. You can only make things out if they're backlighted by the stars or the moon.

In an area where there is high rainfall, where the floors of the forest are always damp or where there are a lot of creepy things that you might not want to deal with at ground level, putting a large hammock up in a tree with a rain covering is the way to go.

When I spent some time in the Everglades, there were strange creepy crawly things on the ground, so I hung a hammock 10 feet high in a tree. In the daytime I could get around by watching where I was going, but at night I would lie in the hammock and just watch the southern parts of the United States come alive.

When you set up your hammock, orient it in a north/south way. Put your head up north, just a little bit higher than your feet; then your circulation will be just about right.

There are many different kinds of hammocks available. Some weigh a little over a pound, roll up into a ball, and fit in your pocket. A rope hammock that has a really wide weave tends to build up pressure spots on certain parts of your body. Too much weight is being supported on too small an area, and therefore things start cutting into your body.

Mexican hammocks that you see with the gaily-colored threads are very comfortable and strong enough to support your weight well, but in a place where there's a lot of rain or heavy dew, they mold and mildew quickly. The $30 or $40 investment that they require will not be justified. Unless you treat them against rot, they will decompose in less than a season if left out in the weather.

The solid hammocks made from one piece of material (canvas or nylon) fill up with water when it rains, and unless you're there to dump the water out, the material will deteriorate. So if you make one out of a solid piece of material, put an eyelet or hole in the center so that if it rains, the water will have a natural leak-place. 22-, 20-, or 18-ounce duck would be a good material. For the rope, get a nylon or polypropylene in a quarter inch thickness or above. When you cut rope it will fray. To keep it from unraveling you could put ends over an open flame or burner and fuse them, whip some thread around them, or tie some tape around them. When you're finished, you will have made yourself a comfortable alternative bed. Happy hanging.

☆ FINISHING ROPE ENDS ☆

for natural fiber ropes

use waxed cotton or linen for whipping (finishing) the line

—Knot

1. sew through rope once.. then wrap thread around rope

A

2. when you reach the end of rope, pull thread tight & sew back through rope to where you started leaving a loop (A) at the unfinished end

3.

A → push this loop down

A

so that the 2 threads cross

A

pull loop over end of rope & pull tight

cut off excess thread here

for nylon & synthetic ropes

hold the end of the rope near a flame & it will melt, fusing the fibers together

TO MAKE A HAMMOCK

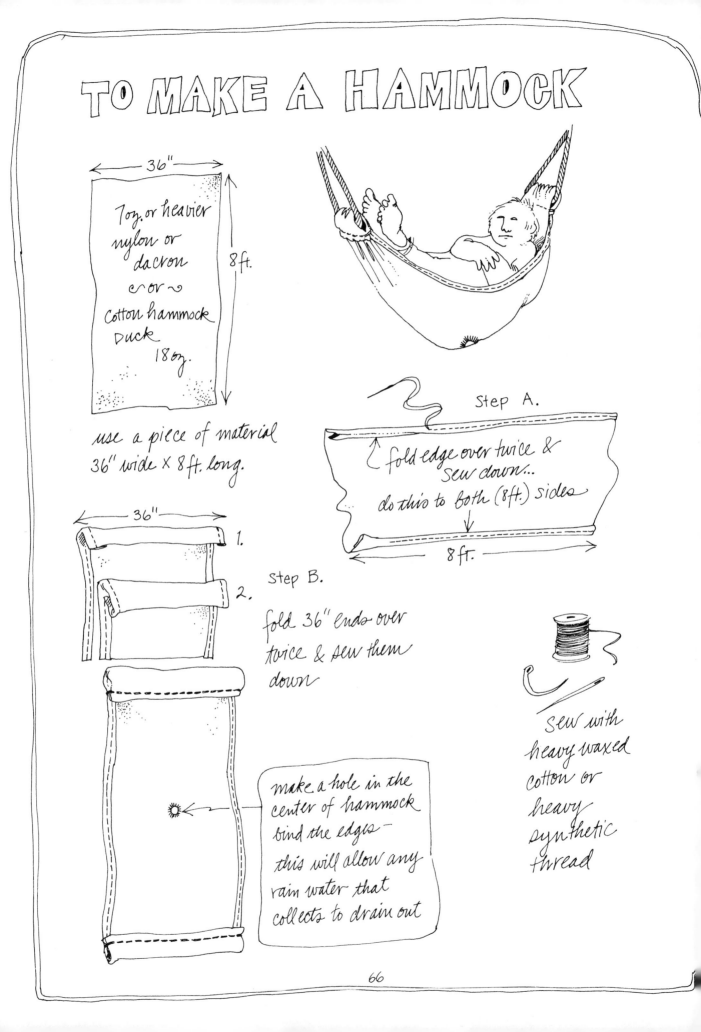

7oz. or heavier nylon or dacron ~or~ cotton hammock DUCK 18oz.

36"

8ft.

use a piece of material 36" wide × 8 ft. long.

Step A.

fold edge over twice & sew down... do this to both (8ft.) sides

8 ft.

36"

1.

2.

Step B.

fold 36" ends over twice & sew them down

make a hole in the center of hammock bind the edges — this will allow any rain water that collects to drain out

sew with heavy waxed cotton or heavy synthetic thread

PERSONAL HYGIENE
& SANITATION

plastic bottle with pop up top

JUST PLAIN SOAP

WASH-ING SODA

a good biodegradable combination

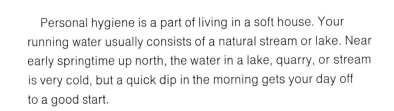

½ to 1 cup soap + ⅓ cup soda

Personal hygiene is a part of living in a soft house. Your running water usually consists of a natural stream or lake. Near early springtime up north, the water in a lake, quarry, or stream is very cold, but a quick dip in the morning gets your day off to a good start.

If you're going to be taking baths in lakes and streams, use a good biodegradable soap. It's better for your body and the water system.

I carry liquid soap in a plastic bottle with a flip top. It's easier to transport than a slippery bar of soap. Even if the bottle is completely filled, it will float.

When I am in the vicinity of a town and want a hot shower or bath, I ride my bicycle from the tent site to a nearby university, college, or high school where there are facilities that can usually be used, either at no cost or for a small fee.

WASHING

put clothes, water,
& soap in pail

use pail with
tight-fitting lid

tie cover on &
secure pail in
your vehicle

clothes slosh around
while you drive,
esp. on the bumps

If you do your laundry by hand you don't have to use soap.
If there's a stream nearby, anchor a piece of clothing down
with a large rock. The running water will get it clean over a
period of hours. Get a plastic barrel with a tight-fitting lid. Put
in some water, some biodegradable soap, and your clothes.
Tie the barrel securely in your vehicle, and as you bounce
around during the course of the day, your clothes will wash
themselves. The soapsuds, if emptied in your garden, will
encourage plant growth.

For health purposes, it is important that all your sanitary
activities be taken care of at least 150 feet from any water
source.

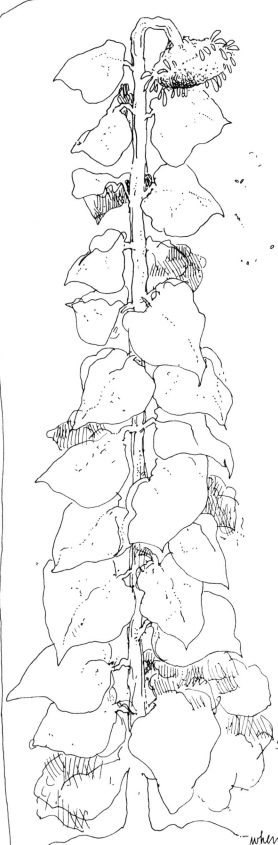

For sanitary purposes, a cupful of ashes or a handful of pine needles effectively sanitizes your latrine site. The ashes will limit the odor and prohibit the attraction of flies. Use the hole until it's filled, then cover it over and plant something there.

Toilet paper is very absorbent. If it's left in the rain even once, it will be useless. I designed a forest-variety toilet-paper dispenser that keeps toilet paper dry, is easily accessible, and easily reloaded. To make it, cut the bottom out of a plastic 1-gallon jug and punch as small a hole as possible in the top for a string to pass through. Next, find a smooth twig about 6 inches long. Tie the string to the middle of the stick and push the stick through the hole in the roll of toilet paper. Fit the stick flat on the bottom of the roll, and break off excess, so the stick is even with the outer-roll diameter. Thread the other end of the string through the jug, and out the hole in the cap. If there's enough excess string, the jug can slide far enough up to change rolls and make it easier to get at the toilet paper. Hang it in a sunny place, because although the paper absorbs moisture, it also dries out rapidly.

when you finish with the hole plant something in it

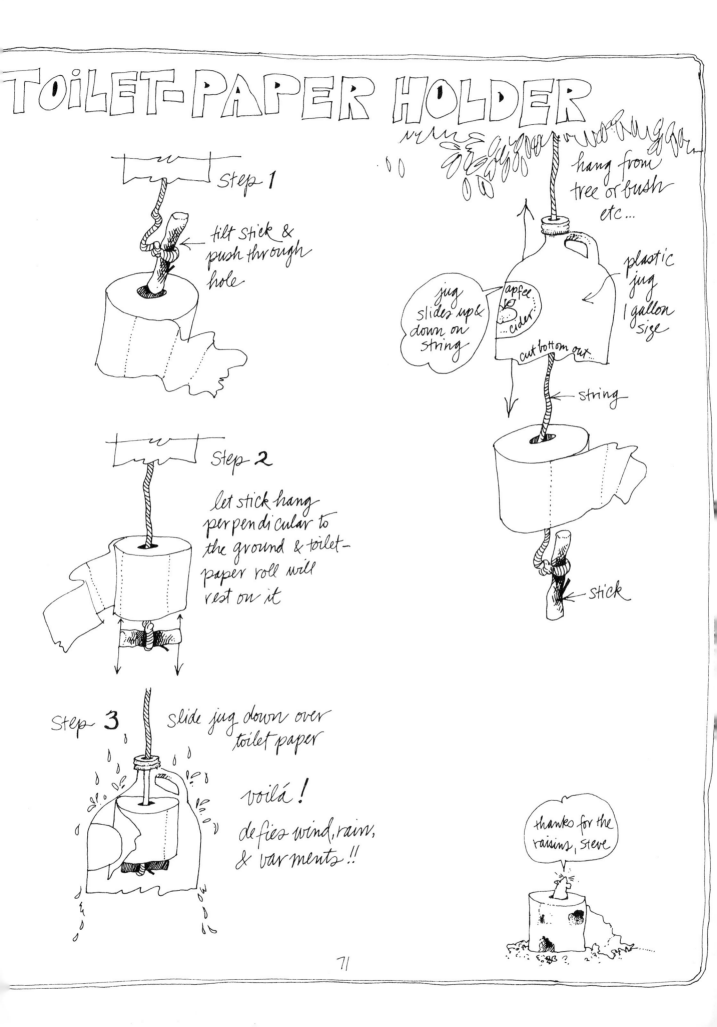

RAISIN

I had a spare roll of toilet paper that I kept on a hanging shelf in a tree. It was under a larger shelf, so it was protected from the rain. My hammock was set up so that while I was lying in it I could see the shelves.

One day while hanging in my hammock, I saw little scraps of toilet paper that had been torn from this roll and spread on the ground. The roll itself looked as if an animal had burrowed into the side of it.

Since I didn't know what kind of animal had done it, I left a peanut and a raisin out, thinking this would determine its species.

I pushed the raisin and the nut in the little hole that the animal had dug. The next day, when I came back to my hammock, I found more toilet paper on the ground, but the raisin and the nut were gone. This continued for several days. The animal kept coming back for its peanut and raisin, and the hole in the toilet paper was almost through the center of the tube.

When I returned next evening, I placed another raisin and nut in the hole. As I lay back in the hammock, I heard some scratching in the tree. I looked up, and saw a mouse. It was climbing along the branches from one tree to another. It crawled into the toilet-paper-roll hole that it had made, dug out a little more, ate the raisin and the nut, then took off through the branches.

When I left at the end of the summer, I put up a fresh roll of toilet paper and all the extra nuts and raisins that I had on hand, and left them as an early Christmas package for the mouse I call Raisin.

OATY

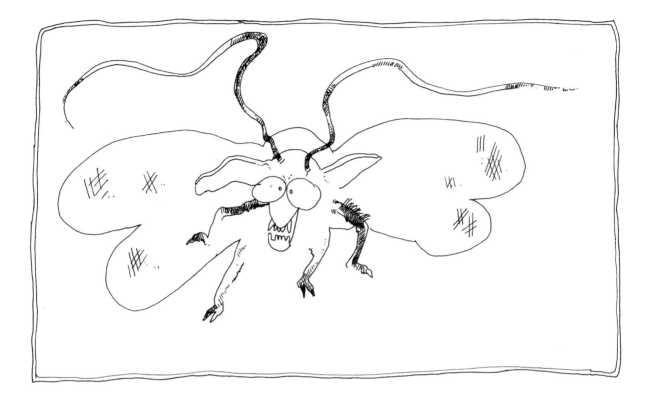

INSECTS

A fox will pick up a stick in its mouth and then swim out into the lake. The fleas on its body walk onto the stick, and when the fox is assured that all the fleas are gone, it lets the stick go and swims back to shore.

I used to wonder why my dog rolled in horse or cow manure, then I realized that she was doing it for a reason. That strong smell acted as an effective insect repellent.

Along the same lines, a friend of mine who grew up in Persia remembered that his people burned cow manure, both for fuel and to repel insects.

In Siberia, the summer tents are like doorless American Indian tipis. There's an outside runged pole that goes up about 20 feet to the smoke hole. Inside there's another ladder that goes down to the ground. The smoke hole is always filled with smoke from something cooking. The rising smoke and the hot air, along with the fact that the door is 18 to 20 feet off the ground, is the way they keep insects out.

Aerosol-spray repellents work well, but they come in pressurized cans, and if they are left in the sun they will explode. They also shouldn't be sprayed on, or near, your tent. There are finishes and chemicals on nylon and cotton that insect sprays will remove; certain materials used in manufacturing clothes are subject to the same ill effects. Our laws are changing the contents from flurocarbon vehicles to CO_2 and so hopefully we will preserve the soft house we live on a little longer.

I've found that although a person's diet doesn't have any effect on the amount of bug bites he or she gets, the kind of soap or perfume used on the body does seem to make a difference.

Our culture has developed varied ways of dealing with bugs. We have exterminators and sophisticated poisons that control them quite well, but I've tried to find how bugs can be dealt with on a natural level.

In ancient cultures, one of the things used was oil of citronella, which is the juice of a grass that grows in Asia and smells like lemons. It's available in almost any drug store, and is quite inexpensive.

Oil of pennyroyal is more difficult to obtain, but is another good insect repellent. It works well on animals too. A little rope collar dipped in either oil and tied around your animal's neck takes away unpleasant animal odors, and also keeps insects away.

If you watch animals, you will see that they've learned to deal with insects in a very natural way.

Everything that is used on your body—from aftershave lotion to underarm spray to feminine hygiene sprays to soap—is perfumed to some degree, and all have an effect on insects. Some of the sweeter-smelling ones attract bees and other insects. I suggest that you use a natural, unperfumed soap.

Probably the only time you will actually want to attract insects is when you're fishing—here's a tip. If you like to fish at night, take a good, stout little candle, and get a flat board that will support the weight of the candle in the water. Melt some wax on the board, and put the candle on it so it sticks. All you have to do is light the candle and float the board out from your boat or the shore (attached by a string), and after a few minutes, the insects will be attracted to the light of the candle. Next, the fish will start to break the surface around the light to get at the insects.

fishing by candlelight

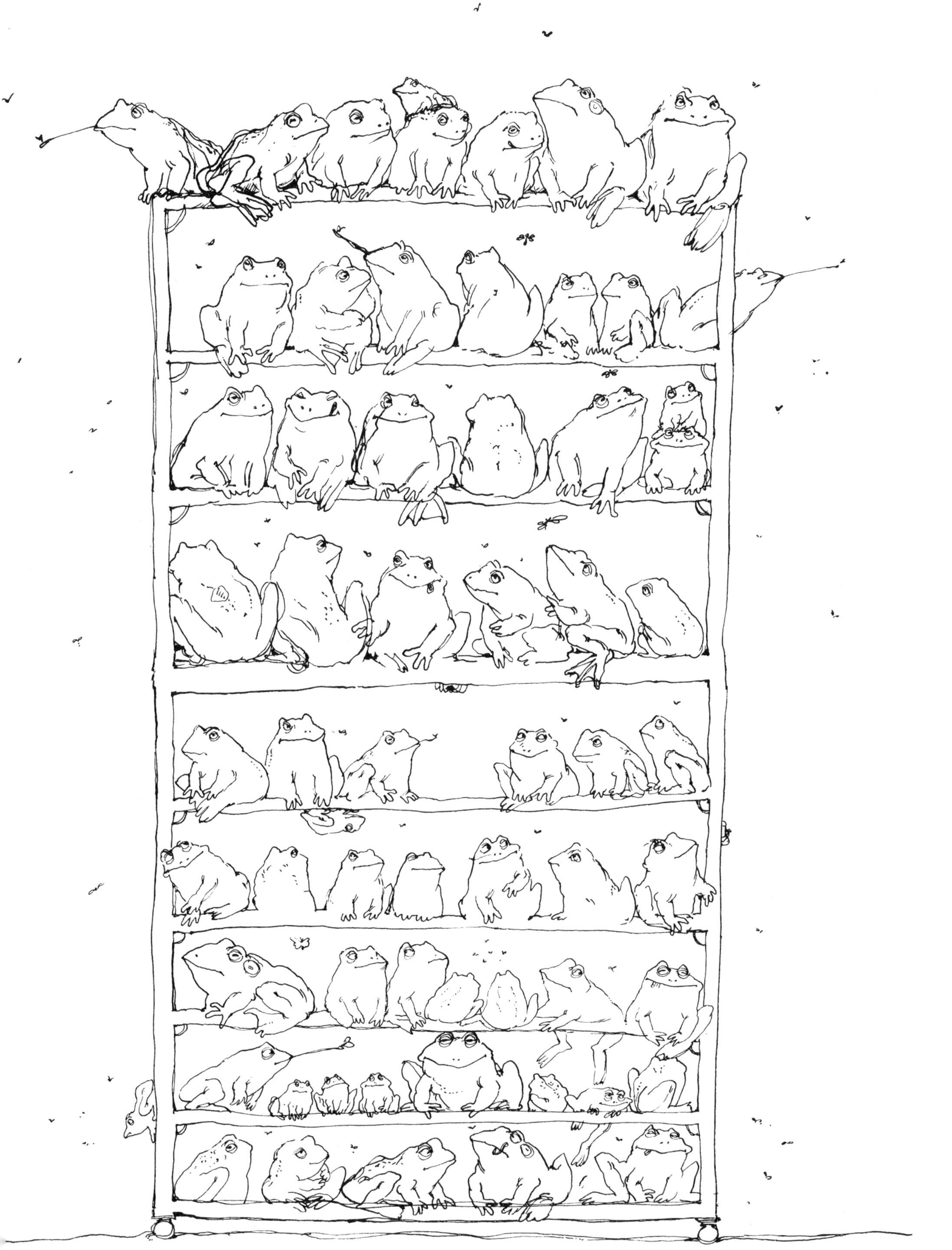

WEATHER

Just as house-structure varies in different parts of the world, depending on the climate, tent design also should evolve according to the local weather.

This summer I lived in a completely transparent tent which I designed and constructed. Everything from lightning bugs to meteor showers—and especially thunder and lightning—was easily visible.

I had a lady friend, Snow White, who was terribly frightened of electric storms. That was the reason she gave for not coming out to my tent. One day, however, she decided she'd be an overnight guest. She made me guarantee that the heavens wouldn't so much as burp that night, and luckily all went well. The next night, as we were sitting on the bed pad, it started to rain. The wind rose, thunder crashed, and the trees began to groan. Suddenly she began to talk nonstop about every thunderstorm she had ever experienced, including the ones in

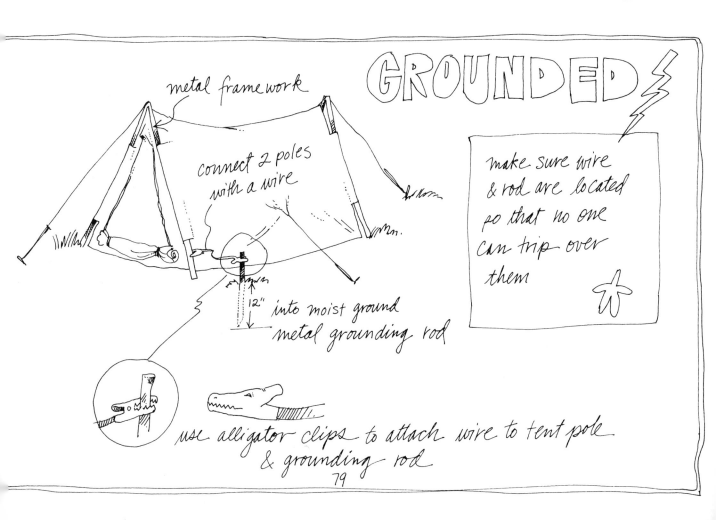

metal framework

GROUNDED

connect 2 poles with a wire

make sure wire & rod are located so that no one can trip over them

12" into moist ground
metal grounding rod

use alligator clips to attach wire to tent pole & grounding rod

her parents' closet. Meanwhile, one of the most ferocious storms I had ever seen was in progress. The wind was really high. One minute it was blowing from one direction, and the next it was blowing from the other. The night was either pitch black, or the whole forest was illuminated in electric white. In the early morning, she was drained from incessant talk, the storm had passed, and we slept.

Lightning should be no cause for worry, provided you take a few precautions. If your tent has a metal skeleton, attach one end of a ground wire to the frame, and the other to a grounding rod, which should penetrate at least a foot down into the moist soil. Remove all jewelry during a storm, and stash it far from your sleeping area. A last bit of advice is never to sleep on the bare floor. Place a closed-cell foam pad between you and the ground. This will effectively insulate you from any lightning that runs across the ground water.

STRANGE NOISES

"snike"
sss

Sometimes an unidentifiable noise will give you the whim whams, or the I'd-rather-be-anywhere-than-here flashes.

One night, my friend Pickett and I were asleep in our tent when she was awakened by a strange clapping sound. Meanwhile, I was asleep and didn't hear anything. Then the Unknown started screeching very loudly, and at that point, I tuned in.

I can remember lying in my sleeping bag, with only one eye showing, looking for the source of the blood-curdling scream—and, on the other, hoping not to find it. I got dressed, and armed with my dog Winnie, I set out to do combat.

white flag

im armed with my trusty dog winnie

Winnie was acting strange. She usually enjoyed an early-morning walk, but not this time. She wanted no part of the trip. I interpreted this as a very bad omen and called off the investigation.

That day, Pickett and I went to some of our country friends and asked what in the world could make a noise like the one we heard. Everybody had lots of scary stories to tell, but none that shed light on our experience.

Later, Pickett and I went back to the tent and walked around looking for signs of the visitor. In our demented minds, the signs could have consisted of anything from broken blades of grass to severed bodies hanging in the trees, or worse. We found nothing.

Part of the experience of camping is unidentified and often untraceable noise, which, once you are used to them, become part of your everyday experience; no different, for example, than the flushing of a toilet or a horn honking outside your house. The normal sixty-cycle hum of electricity in most modern buildings can be more irritating than the noises heard in the woods at night.

BODYGEAR

Since most of your traveling will be done on foot, a discussion on shoes and boots is in order. Many companies are selling very nice, professional-looking climbing and hiking boots. Everyone who wears them seems to have an air of the mountaineer about them, but people who really want to feel the forest use lightweight footwear.

If you're going to be climbing on rough rock surfaces, padded boots are necessary equipment. After the miles start to pile up, though, you're lifting literally tons of extra weight with heavy boots. For general trucking around in the forest, a pair of lightweight shoes will give you a closer feeling for the earth.

I suggest that you get a good-fitting pair of sneakers with a good arch, or a foam pad built into the bottom. Try them on with a pair of heavy socks on your feet. You might need a half or a whole size larger than you'd normally wear.

A pair of sneakers weigh anywhere between 18 and 28 ounces. A pair of decent hiking boots weigh in the 4-pound category.

A good pair of hiking boots runs in the $40 or $50 price range, but if you're going to be doing a lot of climbing, they're an important investment. After wearing heavy boots all day, a pair of sneakers provides you with something light to change into.

There are tread patterns on the bottom of most sneakers. A razor-edged, non-slip pattern is the kind to look for.

A pair of hiking boots that you use in the warmer seasons can temporarily be converted for winter use by cutting out a pair of cardboard innersoles and putting them in the boots to act as insulation.

To minimize tent upkeep, I suggest that you don't wear your shoes inside the tent. Take them off outside and smack them against each other. Make sure that there's nothing sticking to the lugs. Sharp rocks brought into your tent on the bottoms of your shoes could puncture a hole in the floor, and any grit or sand stuck to the soles will act as an abrasive agent and also leave a mess.

Walking in the rain or snow will lose its beauty if your feet are cold and wet. In addition to waterproofing procedures, try taking a plastic bag, slipping it over your socked foot, and then putting on your shoe or boot.

There are many brands of down expedition clothing. The complicated construction used to keep the down in place is very expensive, and as a result, so are all the well-made down products.

There are coats now being made that have closed-cell foam in them (like the pad beneath your sleeping bag) and are less expensive than the down wear. Not only do some of these coats work as Coast Guard-approved life preservers, but they also keep you very warm. They can be purchased in marine clothing stores.

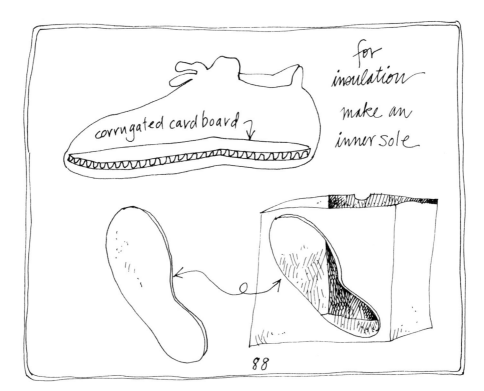

corrugated cardboard

for insulation make an inner sole

88

a big heavy sturdy hiking boot

rocks

poop

gum

sole with lugs
for tread

a sneaker

herring bone tread

WINTER WEAR

Because of cold weather, camping in the winter doesn't sound as enjoyable as camping in the summer, but it does have its own beauty, especially if you are equipped for the cold.

The snow smoothes out all the forest's rough edges, and crunch-walking in the winter stillness is magical.

In the winter, your body needs more food because you use extra energy. The colder it is, the more calories are needed to maintain body temperature.

You also need heavier, insulated clothes to keep you warm. The basic concept of warmth is dependent on the loft which is the dead air space between your body and the outside air. This is created by the insulating material (i.e., down, Fiberfill, Polarguard) used in the garment. The following chart gives a general guideline as to the amount of insulation needed around your body to stay warm at the temperature in the left hand column.

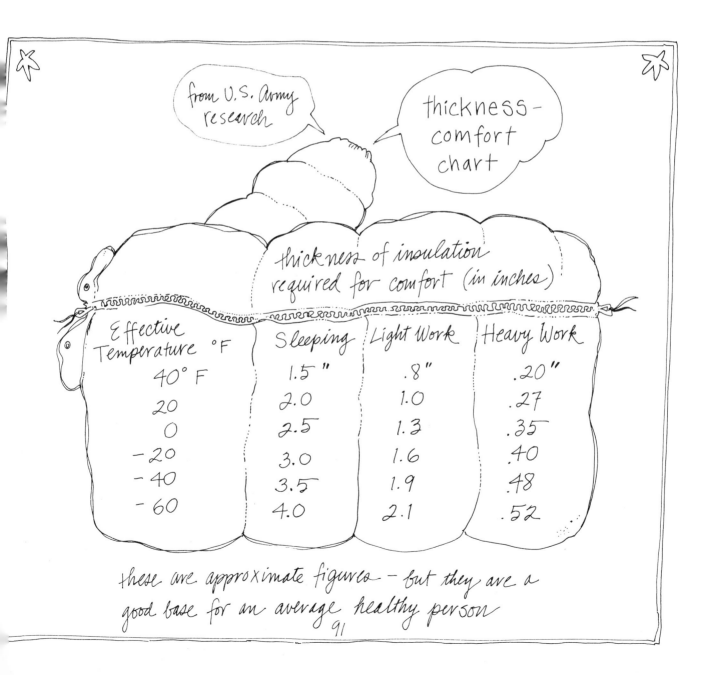

from U.S. Army research

thickness-comfort chart

thickness of insulation required for comfort (in inches)

Effective Temperature °F	Sleeping	Light Work	Heavy Work
40° F	1.5 "	.8 "	.20 "
20	2.0	1.0	.27
0	2.5	1.3	.35
−20	3.0	1.6	.40
−40	3.5	1.9	.48
−60	4.0	2.1	.52

these are approximate figures – but they are a good base for an average healthy person

91

Down, because it's lightweight and has excellent loft for its weight, is very popular. However, nearly any nonconducting fill will give you comparable warmth—even steel wool. The loft is most important.

Wool or polyester are good, less expensive alternatives to down, but the idea behind any of these fabrics is for them to provide layers of dead air and loft between you and the outside.

Hats, hoods, and gloves or mittens are absolutely necessary, because up to 50% of body heat is lost from the neck, face & head area. The best head coverings are the ones which

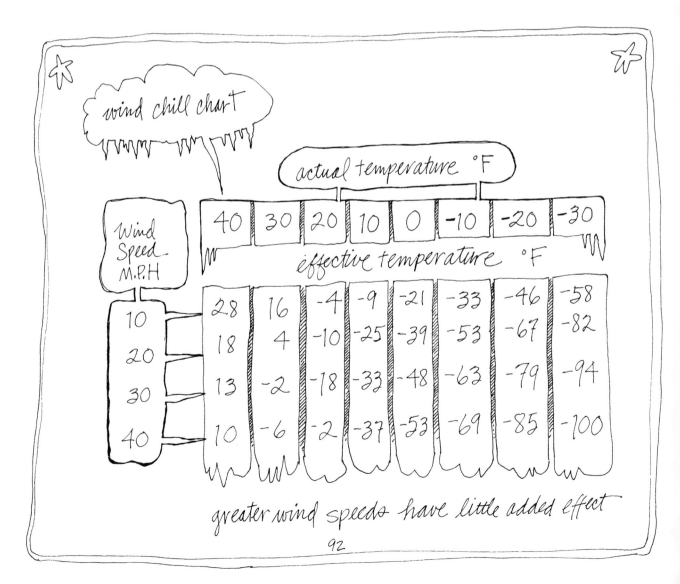

wind chill chart

actual temperature °F

Wind Speed M.P.H	40	30	20	10	0	-10	-20	-30
	effective temperature °F							
10	28	16	-4	-9	-21	-33	-46	-58
20	18	4	-10	-25	-39	-53	-67	-82
30	13	-2	-18	-33	-48	-63	-79	-94
40	10	-6	-21	-37	-53	-69	-85	-100

greater wind speeds have little added effect

have down, polyester, wool or foam liners. For handgear, mittens will keep your fingers much warmer than gloves, because the cold air can't circulate around each separate finger. The wind chill chart tells you how to determine the effective air temperature when the wind is blowing.

In the winter, before you go to bed, it's a good idea to pack your clothes into a stuff sack and put it into the foot area of your sleeping bag. This way your clothes will be warm and dry, and it will make dressing in the morning more comfortable.

put your clothes inside a stuff sack made of breathable material — not a waterproof stuff sack

then keep your clothes inside your bag with you — maybe use them for a pillow — They will be nice & warm come morning

PACKS

Reams of material have been written, and untold amounts of material have been sewn, in an attempt to produce a perfect backpack. It has been my experience that most people's first pack does not suit them, and after living with it for a while and trying on other people's packs, they get a new one that more closely fills their needs and capabilities.

Therefore, when you go to look at packs, I urge you to take along three 10-pound bags of dog food (or reasonable facsimile) and stuff them into any pack you try on. See if the weight carries well, if you can get it on and off OK, and if the whole assembly looks like it can hold the load without coming apart at a point of strain. Most important is that it doesn't give you a high-pressure feeling somewhere on your body.

Wear each pack fully loaded for at least 10 minutes: walk around, kneel, bend over, and just generally give it a chance to annoy you. If it feels like it was made for you, buy it.

Packs are made from the same material as tents are except in a heavier weight. A canvas pack weighs about one-third more than the same pack done in nylon; however, the colors that canvas comes in are more subtle than a lot of the available synthetic colors.

Completely waterproof packs that look like storage boxes with straps are available. If you're doing a lot of wet or water camping, they might suit you.

95

ASSORTED PACKS

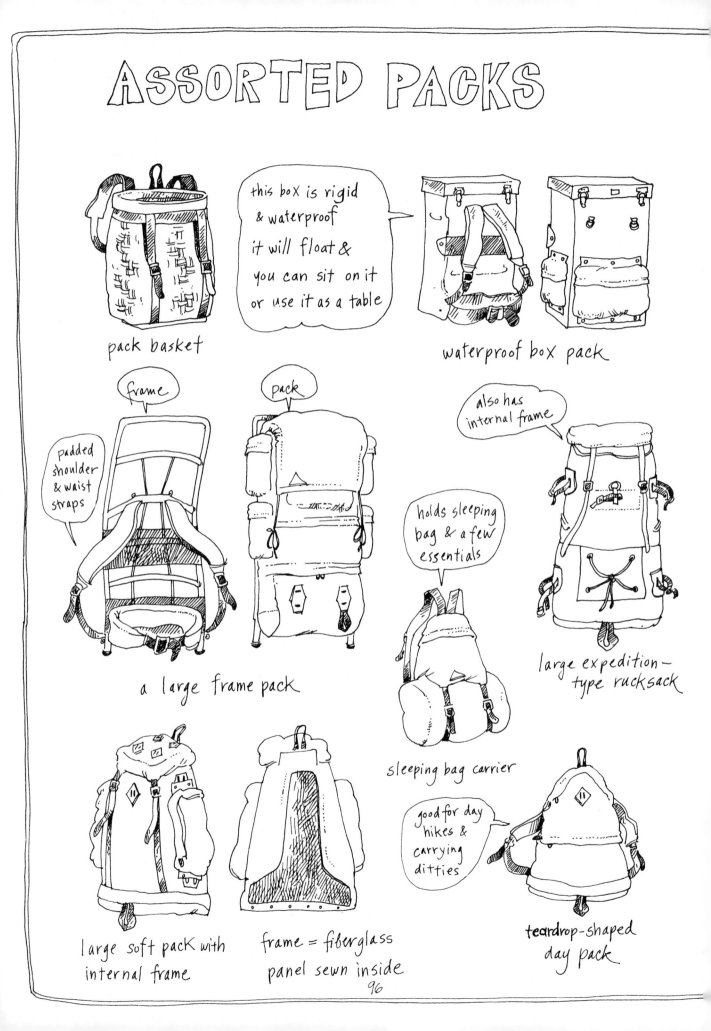

pack basket

this box is rigid & waterproof it will float & you can sit on it or use it as a table

waterproof box pack

frame

pack

also has internal frame

padded shoulder & waist straps

a large frame pack

holds sleeping bag & a few essentials

large expedition-type rucksack

sleeping bag carrier

good for day hikes & carrying ditties

large soft pack with internal frame

frame = fiberglass panel sewn inside

teardrop-shaped day pack

96

If you're into making your own pack, you should use 16-ounce (or heavier) double- or triple-filled canvas, or 8-ounce (or heavier) synthetic. If the material you like is not waterproof you can opt for an assortment of heavyweight plastic, self-sealing bags to carry your stuff in.

A nice, comfortable load to carry will be about one-quarter of your body weight; a little more won't hurt and less is a joy. Aside from all-out expedition work, a bag with around 3000 cubic inches of space inside can carry all you need and you won't feel like a pack animal.

✴ ziploc bags ✴

Bags close this way

10½"

large = 1 gallon

small = 1 quart

11"

8"

7"

for clothes

clean or dirty

socks

one side has a ridge

other side has a groove

for larger sizes, check out suppliers of plastic containers for institutional & industrial use

tea bags

wash cloth

wet or dry

sugar, salt, granola etc.etc

not too good for honey

Packs with external frames are terrible for hitchhiking, so plan accordingly.

If your bucks are down and want a cheap, good pack get an old pair of jeans, sew a few tabs on in the right places, add some rope, an old towel and you're off.

Most metal pack-frames are welded together. If yours breaks, you can use an epoxy glue to put it right, but make sure it is not a water soluable type.

Before heading out, check that all the stuff lashed to the pack is on tight and that the load doesn't stick out wider than your body. Loose stuff will get lost and wide loads just keep getting hung up.

YES

NO

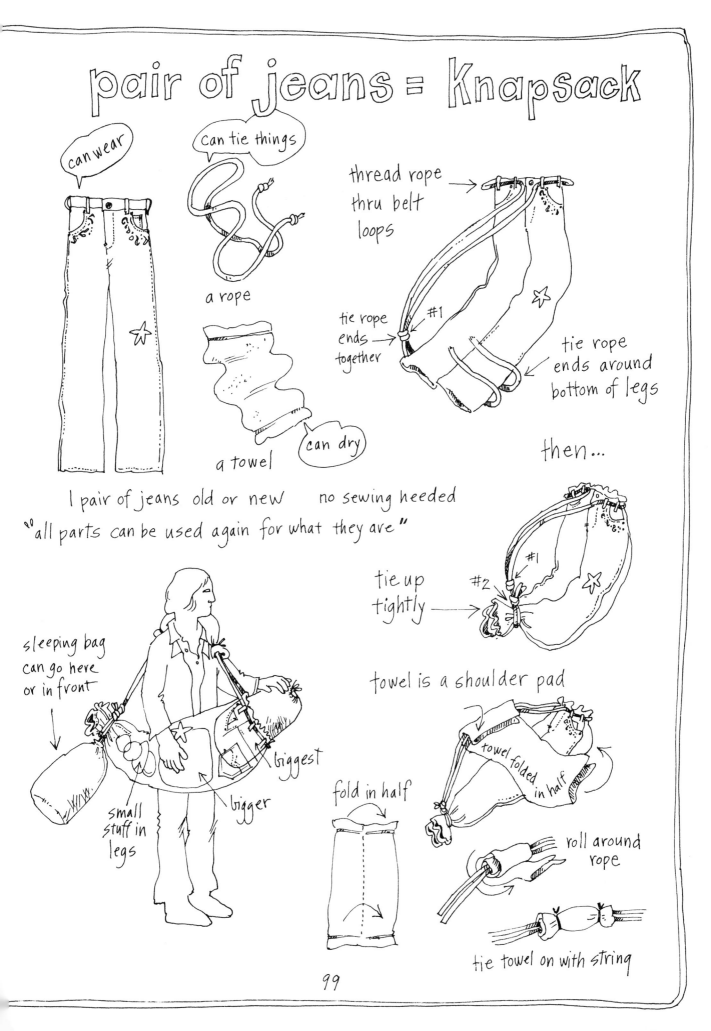

TRAVEL KIT

If you have a car, it's easy to carry more than you need. However, if you're traveling on foot, you'll probably limit yourself to the most needed things.

You should limit your load to 40 pounds, as that is not a large increase over your body weight and won't be a heavy strain to carry.

If you plan carefully, you should be able to fit all the necessary things into a pack and still not exceed the 40-pound limit.

If you take a kit of the following items with you into the woods, your trip will be more successful.

1. A pocket knife. I carry an old U.S. Navy all-stainless-steel four-bladed pocket knife, and I can't remember a day when I haven't used it for something. The edged blade, the awl blade, and the can-opener are always useful.

2. Needles. I have a whole assortment of sailmaker's needles from the small to the very largest, which will penetrate leather or heavy canvas. Also, I carry an assortment of small darning needles for socks, etc.

3. Thread. There are several kinds of thread I recommend. One is a very tightly woven cotton thread with a waxed coating on it. It's heavy, nearly waterproof, and is good for sewing dungarees, jackets, tents, and hammocks. Another good thread is a cotton-outercore thread, with a polyester or nylon innercore. The cotton around the innercore of polyester swells when it gets wet, and provides natural waterproof abilities while the innercore provides strength.

4. Extra stakes. If you're in a place where you can't find dead branches and you have to carry your stakes with you, take a couple of extra ones. Stakes are easily lost.

5. Candles. Candles work well as emergency lights. Another use for a candle is in waterproofing. Wax can be dripped on a cotton tent where you have holes, and even if the tent happens to be wet, it will cover them. An interesting thing about wax is that when the sun comes out and the top of the tent gets really warm, the wax will melt down into the hole and make an excellent fix. So, even if you can't get it on too neatly when you first apply it, the sun will take care of it for you. Candles will melt in your pack, causing a mess, if your pack is left in the sun. Carry them by themselves in a plastic bag.

6. Safety pins. If you carefully place a safety pin through the inside seam area of your tent, without it piercing the outer coating, you can put a light string on it and hang a wash cloth or other fairly light, nice-to-have-around things.

7. A flashlight. Preferably, try and get the pencil type of flashlight. It uses two (AA) cells and weighs about 3 ounces fully loaded. It costs $2.00 retail, batteries included. It has a clip on it that can be attached to your pocket. It's not waterproof, but could be made so by putting silicone caulking seal on it.

8. Rope. Rope is a basic fastening device, and is necessary when you're living outside. Rope is designed with stretch, some with more of an elongation factor than others. I like the idea of using natural and organic ropes, but I find that in a place where there's a lot of rain or dampness, they rot, mildew, and lose their strength rapidly. Synthetic ropes (especially polyethylene), on the other hand, are nonabsorbant.

9. A radio. Having a radio in your tent will keep you in touch with the outside world. You can listen to music, or find out how the weather will be. If you're moving around, a little AM/FM portable weighs only a pound with batteries in it. Many companies make small units in which a cassette recorder, player, and AM/FM radio are built together. They weigh around 7 pounds. Some have adapters that work off 6- or 12-volt car batteries, and some 117-volt adapters so they can be used in your home.

10. Batteries. If you are taking battery-powered articles with you, try to select ones that use the same type of battery. This would allow you to replace dead batteries with live ones if your flashlight gives out on a dark night. It is worth the extra money to invest in long-life batteries, as they do last considerably longer than the inexpensive ones.

THINGS TO TAKE

tetnus injection & other shots where necessary

handkerchief

extra pair glasses

Sunglasses

money — cash or travelers checks

extra contact lenses

keep all important papers in one place — a waterproof envelope is best

prescription drugs

TRAVEL KIT

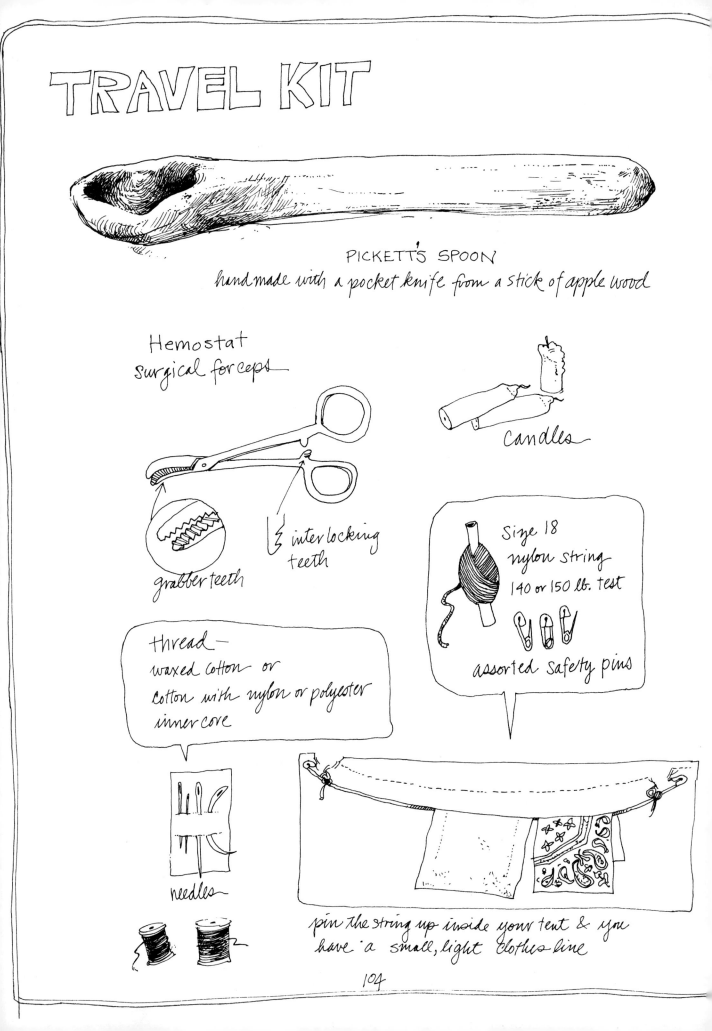

PICKETT'S SPOON
hand made with a pocket knife from a stick of apple wood

Hemostat
surgical forceps

interlocking teeth

grabber teeth

candles

Size 18
nylon string
140 or 150 lb. test

assorted safety pins

thread—
waxed cotton or
cotton with nylon or polyester
inner core

needles

pin the string up inside your tent & you
have a small, light clothes line

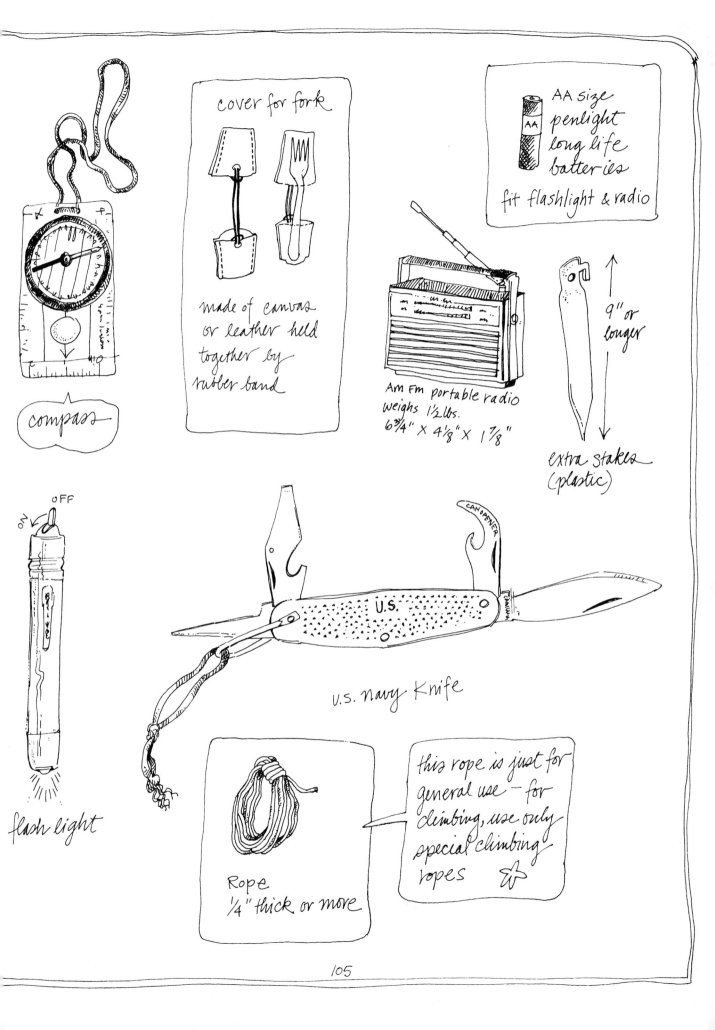

compass

cover for fork

made of canvas
or leather held
together by
rubber band

AA size
penlight
long life
batteries

fit flashlight & radio

AM FM portable radio
weighs 1½ lbs.
6¾" X 4⅛" X 1⅞"

9" or
longer

extra stakes
(plastic)

OFF
ON

U.S.

CAN OPENER

U.S. navy knife

flash light

Rope
¼" thick or more

this rope is just for
general use — for
climbing, use only
special climbing
ropes

40 lb. soft household

personal stuff for knapsack

good for weather down to 0°F

10. wooden spoon
Stainless steel fork
Chop sticks

11. medicine prescription drugs
insect repellent   oil of citronella

12. Sunglasses

13. extra glasses or contact lenses

1. Rain Poncho large size

vizor

extra-long back to cover pack

hood

14. film can w/ fish hooks & nuts & bolts for sinkers   FILM

15. MIRROR — polished metal for seeing yourself & signaling

CARRY-ING CASE

2. Hammock

3. 15 ft. × 15 ft.
6 MIL or thicker clear plastic tarp for tent or lean to

4. Soap in plastic bottle   SOAP

5. canteen

6. pocket knife   US

7. sewing kit

8. Compass

9. string

16. Heavy duty food storage bags
11½" × 13" or larger

17. Monofilament line — small spool
50 yds   15 lb. test
for fishing

18. CLOTHES

extra socks

extra long pants

Shorts

cotton gloves

long johns

extra underpants if you wear them

tee shirts

shirt

turtle neck shirt

hooded sweatshirt

sweater

handker-chief

razor ??

hair brush

tooth brush & tooth paste. BLASTO

a hat

19. Closed cell foam pad - for mattress (ie Ensolite)

20.

21. COOKING

2 qt. measuring cup for mixing & cooking — metal

22. 7 oz. can Sterno with holder

23. 2½ lb. box of dog food & pets' travel kit

DOG FOOD

that is if you have a pet traveling with you

24. cigarette lighter &/or matches

matches in plastic bag

SURVIVAL

newspaper makes good insulation

When I taught a survival course (at a private school) I surprised people by coming into the class one day and telling them "We're going out until the next morning; let's go." Everyone wanted to stop by the kitchen or pick up their sleeping bags, etc. . . . and I said, "Nope, we go as we are."

Survival is an attitude. If it happens that you will be put in a survival situation, it will be without much advance notice, so you have to make do with what is on hand.

Your objective is to keep the human motor running until such time as the imminent danger is past (rescue). To do this you must keep your body at as comfortable a temperature as possible, regardless of the air temperature, while expending the least amount of energy.

In cold weather, during periods of strenuous activity, your body can consume 6,000 calories a day. It will be near impossible to replace that calorie level under most survival conditions. So slow down and burn 3,000 calories per day and live twice as long. Don't drink cold fluids either, as it takes your body lots of heat to warm the fluid up to your body's temperature after you swallow it. Put the fluid container next to your body and let it heat by the body warmth given off, then drink it.

NO SWEAT

You can go for a few weeks without food. However, water is a must or you'll perish in a few days. In cold weather you need just as much fluid as in warm weather because for your body to give off heat it must give off water vapor as well. Figure on half a gallon of fluid per day, minimum.

Use your head: it's a lot better to sit in one place and decide your moves when you're as together as you can be than to run around and go nowhere with no plan.

There are many cases of totally untrained and unprepared people who survived for very long periods because they used their heads and made do. There are also many cases of highly trained, well-prepared people who failed after a few days because they weren't thinking. So be resourceful: think and survive.

Once there was a guy named Skrewy... he lived in Detroit and managed a psycedelic rock and roll band... he didn't really live anywhere ...so after a hard night he would crawl into the nearest Goodwill box for warm dry sleep.

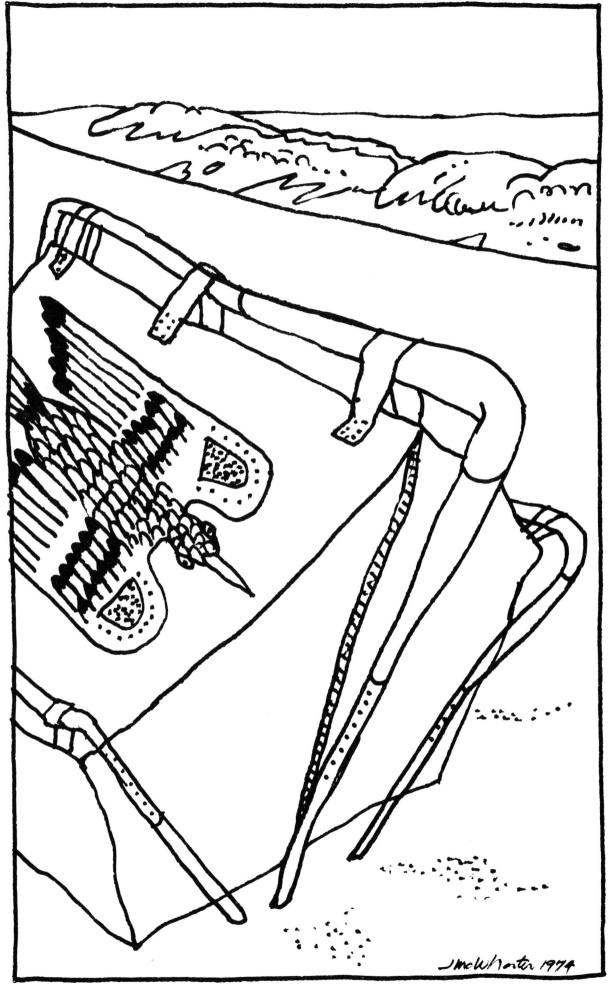

Bruce McDonald

Bruce McDonald

James A. Smith

James A. Smith

Jane McWhorter

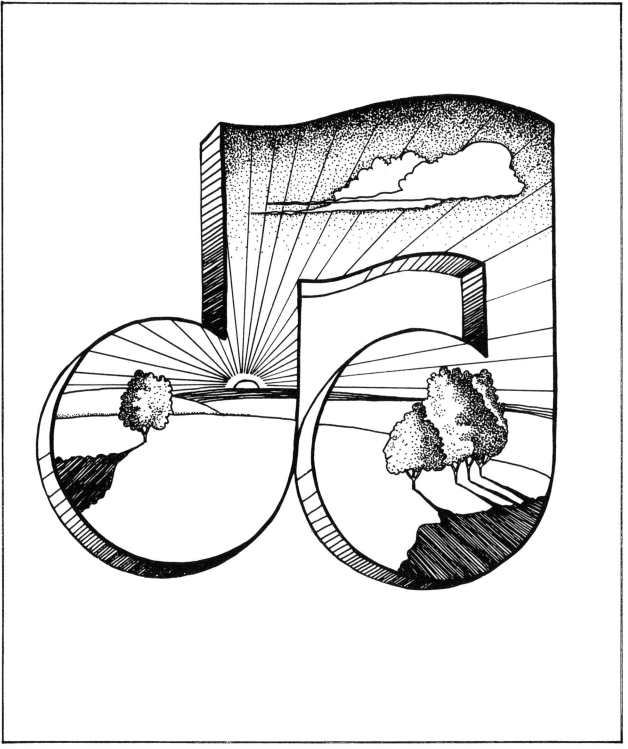

Lee Goldstein

McWhorter
1974

118

Jason McWhorter

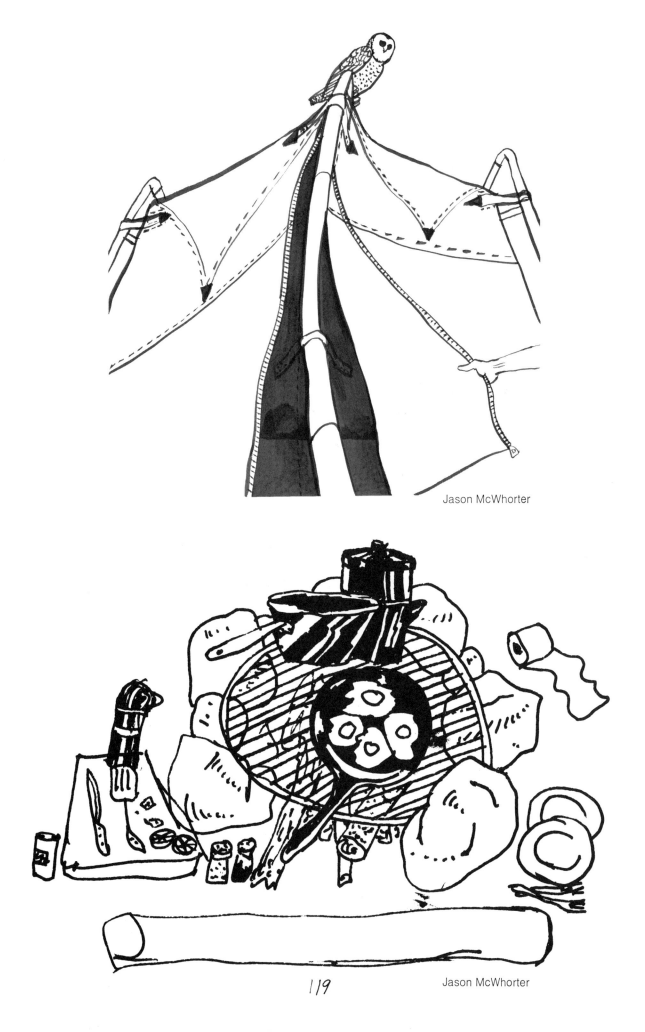

Jason McWhorter

119

Jason McWhorter

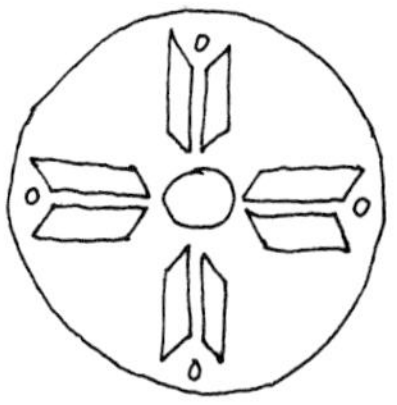

Good medicine ... tipi makers

Leaving our tipis
    for a walk in the woods
        to a wonderful stream
    running
      whooping
        hiding behind trees
          sneaking up on each other

    swimming in a mountain stream
      dancing on the rocks
        lying under the waterfall
          in the pocket of air

  laughing shouting
      drumming on the rocks

Then down stream again
    to the river
      and the tipis
        and warm fires.

We make tipis because they are beautiful
    beautiful glowing radiant teachers
        teachers of Indian life
           and heart
           and soul
           and mind.

We make tipis because they are homes
    and everybody's got to have a home
        'cause home is the place of love and family
           and the center of the whole world.

We make tipis because they are temples
    temples of the out-of-doors
        temples of the circle
           and the fire in the center.

We make tipis because we love to sew
    strong straight honest seams
        hard worked eyes
  made with pride
    and joy
        with prayers
          and best wishes
  and with praise to the Lord.

David Woodsfellow, Good Medicine Tipi makers

we wish you a
Merry Christmas
and a
Happy New
Year

Dave, Ann, & Sky at
Good Medicine

Annie Woodsfellow

Karl Dastoli

apple

/23

Margot Apple

steve's kitchen in the woods ...

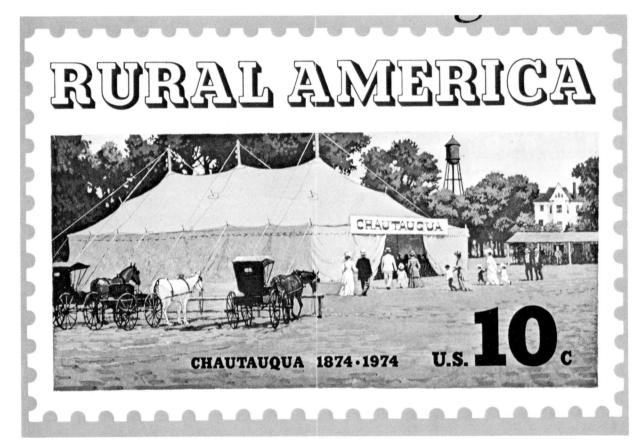

U.S. Postal Service

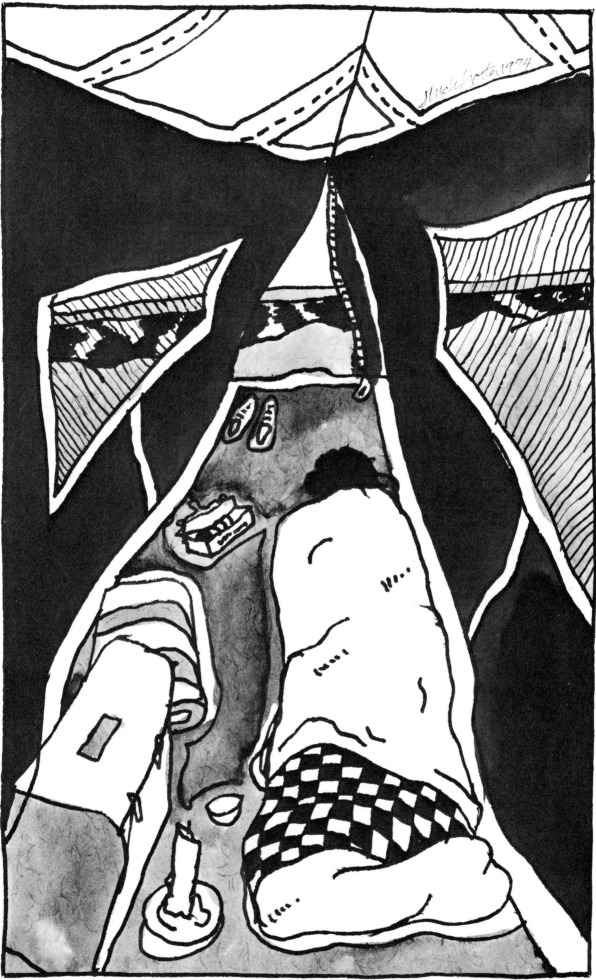

Jason McWhorter

WEIGHTS & MEASURES

CONVERSION TABLE FOR METRIC EQUIVALENTS

	US	METRIC
1 acre	43,560 sq ft	40.4687 ares
are	119.6 sq yd/.02471 acre	100 sq m
board foot	144 cu in	.00236 cu m
bolt	40 yd	36.58 m
bushel	32 dry qt/2150.42 cu in	35238.89 cc
centimeter	.3937 in	.01 m
square centimeter	.155 sq in	.0001 sq m
cubic centimeter	.0610 cu in	.001 l
cord	128 cu ft	3.625 cu m
decimeter	3.937 in	.1 m
fathom	6 ft	1.829 m
fluid ounce	$1/16$ pt	29.6 cc
foot	12 in	30.48 cm
square foot	144 sq in	929 sq cm
cubic foot	1728 cu in	28.317 cu dm
furlong	220 yd	201.17 m
gallon	231 cu in	3.7853 l
hank	840 yd	768.1 m
hogshead	63 gal	238.5 l
inch	$1/12$ ft	2.54 cm
square inch	$1/144$ sq ft	6.452 sq cm
cubic inch	$1/1728$ cu ft	16.387 cc
kiloliter	264.18 gal	1000 l
kilometer	.62137 mi	1000 m
square kilometer	.3861 sq mi/247.104 acres	10,000 ares
liter	1.0567 liq qt	1000 cc
meter	39.370113 in	100 cm
square meter	1.1960 sq yd	.01 are
cubic meter	1.308 cu yd	1000 l
mile	5,280 ft/1760 yd	1609.3 m
square mile	640 acres	2.5900 sq km
millimeter	.03937 in	.001 m
ounce	$1/16$ lb	29.6 cc
peck	$1/4$ bushel/537.61 cu in	8.8096 l
pint	16 oz (dry)	.551 l
quart	32 oz (dry)	1.101 l

LINEAR MEASURES

12 in = 1 ft
3 ft = 1 yd
144 sq in = 1 sq ft
9 sq ft = 1 sq yd
640 acres = 1 sq mi.

LIQUID MEASURE

16 oz = 1 pt
2 pt = 1 qt
4 qt = 1 gal
31½ gal = 1 barrel
2 bar = 1 hogshead

APOTHECARIES FLUID MEASURE

60 minims = 1 dram
8 drams = 1 oz
16 oz = 1 pint
2 pts = 1 qt
4 qts = 1 gal

DRY MEASURE

grain = 7,000 to the lb avoirdupois
        5,760 to the Troy lb & apothecaries lb
1 grain = .0648 gram
1 gram = 15.432 grains

TEMPERATURES

32° F (water freezes) is equal to 0° C.
212° F (water boils) is equal to 100° C.

GLOSSARY

Alloy—a mating of 2 or more materials for increased performance in a given function or to save costly materials by mixing with more inexpensive materials to incorporate the costly materials' attributes.

Barometer—an instrument for determining the pressure of the surrounding atmosphere, for judging the probable changes of weather, and for determining the height of an ascent. Invented in 1643 in Florence, Italy, by Evangelista Torricelli, one of Galileo's assistants. At sea level, the ordinary reading will be approximately 30 inches of mercury.

BTU (British Thermal Unit)—the quantity of the heat required to raise the temperature of 1 pound of water 1° Fahrenheit, at or near its maximum density.

Calorie—the amount of heat required at a pressure of 1 atmosphere (14.7 lb per sq in) to raise the temperature of 1 gram of water 1° Centigrade. The statement that a tablespoon of honey contains about 100 calories means that, when oxidized in the body, it will release about that much heat energy for muscular or other bodily activities.

Candlepower—luminous intensity. More candlepower means brighter light, usually with higher fuel consumption.

Denier—a unit of weight expressing the fineness of yarn, expressed in grams per 9,000 meters of length.

Elongation—the difference between a material under no tension and its give when the rupture point is reached.

Hand—the feeling of a rope or woven material as to its ease of workability, or resistance of workability.

Horsepower—a unit of power. One horsepower is the energy needed to lift 33,000 pounds 1 foot in 1 minute.

Tensile Strength—the greatest stress in the long direction before a substance will part. It is expressed as pounds per square inch, or kilograms per square centimeter.

Warp—the lengthwise arrangement of yarns into a woven pattern.

RESOURCES

The rating system at the end of each item in the resource section pertains to the informational level of the publication, not the products.

ALPINE DESIGN, A GENERAL RECREATION, INC., CO.
1685 East Parpahoe
P. O. Box 3407
Boulder, Colo. 80303

Tents, down clothing and packs. Their packbound poncho is one of the better designs of its kind. Ideal for groundcloth, poncho, and shelter. Covers both you and your pack when you're on the trail. Weighs 1 pound, 5 ounces. Good.

AMERICAN NATIONAL STANDARDS INSTITUTE
1430 Broadway
New York, N.Y. 10018

A catalogue of catalogues which offers a wide variety of how-to books on tent procedures and results on the following subjects: textiles, tents, fireproofing, solar energy, water penetration, adhesives, tablecloths, water coolers, waste disposers, space heating devices, etc. This is the most complete catalogue I have ever seen. It can be used to order books on literally any subject of interest. Excellent.

CELANESE FIBERS MARKETING CO.
1211 Ave. of the Americas
New York, N.Y. 10036
Att: Jerry Emeret, Director, Fiberfill Sales

Informational brochure on Polarguard, a man-made insulation that is receiving a lot of attention from cold-weather-equipment manufacturers. Its main strength is that it insulates while wet, cannot absorb moisture, and can be used without the more expensive construction techniques which are needed when you are working with down. Polarguard is superior to down if wet-weather camping is anticipated; canoe and kayak campers, for instance, use Polarguard. This particular brochure is only slightly informative, but new ones may exist. Also, more information can be obtained from companies who make ski clothes and sleeping bags.

CELANESE FIBERS MARKETING CO.
1211 Ave. of the Americas
New York, N.Y. 10036
Att: Coordinator, Information Services

A booklet (with samples) which contains information on the characteristics, uses, and care of fabrics containing Arnel triacetate. Information useful for both tent- and clothing-design possibilities. Good.

CHAMPION INDUSTRIES
35 East Poplar St.
Philadelphia, Pa. 19123

This catalogue includes imported and domestic camping and recreational supplies. From lamps to berets, from stoves to foot pumps, from sleeping bags to bicycling supplies—a little bit of almost everything! Army mosquito headnets, wood-burning stoves (at very low prices), immersion heaters, para-chutes, all forms of gas masks and rocketbags—"2-Man English Bivouac tents, made to withstand the sands of El Alamein"! Excellent. Catalogue price: $1.00

DEFENDER INDUSTRIES
255 Main St.
New Rochelle, N.Y. 10801

Complete buyer's guide for marine goodies. Includes hard-ware and soft goods built to withstand the harshest environ-ments. Many products here will be very useful for both campers and those who wish to design their own tents. Sailcloth comes in a variety of weights and materials: nylon, Dacron, poly-ethylene, doublefill canvas, hammock duck, etc. Excellent. Catalogue price: $1.00

DOME EAST CORP.
325 Duffy Ave.
Hicksville, N.Y. 11801

A catalogue of sizes and capabilities of domes covered with a plastic skin. Tells what can be done in terms of design— recommended for anyone who wants to make their own tent, dome, or other dwelling. Good.

EASTERN MOUNTAIN SPORTS, INC.
1041 Commonwealth Ave.
Boston, Mass 02215

A very comprehensive catalogue, fully descriptive and pictorial from the country's largest retailer of cross-country skis. The catalogue offers a wide variety of tent designs, packs, camp stoves, collapsible toothbrush kits, climbing hardware, emergency items, underwear, etc. Excellent. Catalogue price: $1.00

EDDIE BAUER, EXPEDITION OUTFITTERS
P. O. Box 3700
Seattle, Washington 98124

Extensive line of clothing made entirely by Bauer or according to their specifications. Clothes especially suited to people working in cold northern regions. Parkas from $-80°$ to $40°$ above. Down gloves, boots, vests, sleeping bags, hats . . . Excellent.

EUREKA TENT CO.
625 Conklin Rd.
Binghamton, N.Y. 13903

One of the manufacturers of large family style tents; their Blanchard designs being among the best. Excellent.

GERRY
5450 No. Valley Highway
Denver, Colo. 80216

An old-line company of mountaineering products. Each and every catalogue contains much information on tents, insulation,

and other pertinent information for campers and backpackers.
Excellent. Also available: "How to Enjoy Backpacking," "How
To Camp and Leave No Trace," "How To Keep Warm." All
three excellent booklets, written by Gerry Cunningham, may
be obtained free by writing to the above.

GOOD MEDICINE TIPI MAKERS
Main St.
Cambridgeport, Vermont 05141
(802) 869-2672

Informative flyer on tipis, which they make from natural
materials and with hand stitching. All tents made to order in
sizes ranging from 12 to 22 feet in diameter. Designs based
on the Sioux tipi. Good.

Workshops are given where you can make a tipi with your
own hands. The cost, not including materials, for two weeks
is $100 per person or $150 for you and a friend. Bring your
own bedding and food. For more info call: (802) 869-2672.

HUNTER OUTDOOR PRODUCTS INC.
234 Union St.
North Adams, Mass. 01247

Designers of Army mobile operating-room tents, which are
inflatable. The company has no desire to make high-technology
tents for the public. Catalogue does not include military tent-
making techniques or their features, just their inexpensive, but
average-in-quality consumer line. Bad.

JANSPORT
Painefield Industrial Park
Everett, Washington 98204

A catalogue containing information on the manufacturers of
some of the most advanced designs in domes, backpacks, and
tents, including one of the few tents that uses the advantages
of ripstop Dacron. These tents can be moved from place to
place, fully assembled. A four- to six-person tent weighs under
13 pounds total. Backpacks are designed for both city and
expedition use. Excellent.

KELTY PACK, INC.
10909 Tuxford St.
P. O. Box 639
Sun Valley, Ca. 91352

Mainly featuring packs by a designer who has been doing trend-setting work since the early 1950s; also down clothing. Excellent.

KENYON INDUSTRIES
5714 Empire State Building
350 Fifth Ave.
New York, N.Y. 10018

Catalogue describing Kenyon Industries' processing of quality fabrics. Kenyon K-Kote is a versatile fabric finish which is water-resistant and can be tailored to a wide number of uses —for instance, Super K-Kote is a clear, heavy coating for maximum water resistance. LT K-Kote is a light coating for water resistance. All are washable and dry-cleanable. Recommended for those interested in tent/clothing design. Good.

KENYON PIECE DYEWORKS, INC.
Kenyon, Rhode Island 02836

They have many informational catalogues on dealing with manmade fabrics and fibers. Especially recommended is their Flame-Retardant Processing Kit, which includes treating, processing, and testing techniques in fireproofing, down proofing, and weather resistance, with a glossary of all technical terms on the above subjects. This is especially important reading for anyone who is concerned with fireproofing. Excellent.

KLEIN'S
Dept. 720
185 N. Wabash Ave.
Chicago, Ill. 60601

A catalogue of sporting-goods items, mainly featuring fishing equipment, but also including an assortment of both Klein's and Coleman outdoor items—lanterns, heaters, coolers, tents, backpacks, sleeping bags, etc. Excellent.

MARINE VELCRO DIVISION
P. O. Box 694
Pratt St. & Boston Post Rd.
New Rochelle, N.Y. 10801

A brochure advertising over 101 interesting boating applications of Velcro tapes: coiling ropes, tying down gear on deck
in any weather, holding anchors safely in place, holding down
boat carpets, keeping bunk cushions and blankets in place.

MOUNTAIN SAFETY RESEARCH, INC.
So. 96th St. at 8th Ave.
South Seattle, Washington 98108

Mountain Safety publishes an excellent newsletter for testing
situations: hiking, camping, and mountain climbing. There is
also a catalogue of equipment designed for the serious backpacker. For both newsletter and catalogue subscription, send
$5.00 with your name and address to the above address.
Excellent, but designed for the serious climber or backpacker.

NETCRAFT CO.
3101 Sylvania
Toledo, Ohio 43613

Outstanding do-it-yourself catalogue for ropes, netting, shut-
ters, all equipment needed for making hammocks, fishnets,
handbags, laundrybags. Netcraft also sells books on the subject
of netcraft: *How To Trap Fish and Turtles, Trapping North
American Furbearers,* etc. They specialize in make-your-own
tackle, lures, rods. Excellent.

THE NORTH FACE
1234 Fifth St.
Berkeley, Ca. 94710

Expedition-quality tents, packs and clothes. Aside from fine
down products, they make one of the best synthetically-filled
sleeping bags on today's market. Very informative as to care
and proper use of equipment. Excellent.

PUTNAM MILLS CORP.
49 West 37th St.
New York, N.Y. 10018

A folding brochure of swatches of nylon in a rainbow assortment of colors, from burgundy to Haitian pink and from Rum gold to Dublin green. The important factor here is that most tents made of nylon only come in blue and orange. Excellent.

RECREATIONAL EQUIPMENT, INC.
1525 11th Ave.
Seattle, Wash. 98122

This catalogue on complete camping and climbing accessories is large and varied. Recreational Equipment, Inc. is a co-op which operates on the Rochdale plan: one rate of patronage dividend to the members based on purchases. It includes safety and equipment-care instructions as well as exhibits an enormous line of fine products. Excellent.

SIERRA DESIGNS
4th & Addison Streets
Berkeley, Ca. 94710

Informational and pictorial flyer of limited but fine offerings: sleeping bags, packs, goosedown clothing, mountain parkas, and tents. Excellent.

TIPI MAKERS
339 15th St.
Shoppe 150
Oakland, Ca. 94612

Complete description of tipis and their evolution, illustrated with photographs and drawings. Descriptions of natural-fiber tipi materials, including information on pegs, poles, stitching, ground covers, etc. Excellent.

VELCRO CORP.
681 Fifth Ave.
New York, N.Y. 10022

A technical manual explaining the practical applications of
Velcro Hook and Loop Tapes, which are "snagproof, jamproof,
lightweight, washable and dry-cleanable." The manual is de-
voted to sewing techniques, but tapes can also be adhered
by adhesive, heat-sealing methods, nails, or staples. Durable
through thousands of opening and closing cycles. This is a
must for anyone who wishes to improve on the design of tent
doors, windows, etc. Good.

WINSLOW CO. MARINE PRODUCTS
P. O. Box 578
Osprey, Fla. 33559

Informational flyer advertising Winslow self-erecting en-
closed life rafts holding up to twelve persons. Protective canopy
will maintain bodily warmth in cold climates. Here is the basis
for a good floating tent design. Good.

YKK CREATIVE GROWTH '73 '74 or '75
Valley Brook Rd.
Lyndhurst, N.J. 07071
Att: D. Carmichael, Marketing Mgr.

Contains the complete design and manufacturing capabilities of the largest zipper manufacturer in the world. Good.

MAGAZINES AND REPRINTS

American Forests—Who's managing our forests and how. With lots of pretty pictures. 12 issues a year, $7.50
The American Forestry Association, 1319 18th St. NW, Washington, D.C. 20036

Ascent—One issue per year, $6.00. Sierra Club, 1050 Mills Tower, San Francisco, Ca. 94104

Back Packer—From Backpacker, Inc. 4 copies a year at $2.50 per copy, or $7.50 per year. 28 W. 44th St., N.Y., N.Y. 10036

Farm Journal—If you really want to know how your food is grown, it's a bargain. $2.00 per year (11 copies) from Farm Journal, Inc., Washington Square, Philadelphia, Pa. 19105

Manmade Fibers, 1974 Deskbook—A reprint from the March 1974 issue of *Modern Textiles.* It contains the essential information about U.S. manmade fibers, including a description of properties and end uses and a list of all the fibers and who makes them. $2.00 each, from Modern Textiles Magazine, 303 Fifth Ave., N.Y., N.Y. 10016

INDEX